CRISIS AND RECOVERY

CRISIS AND RECOVERY

ETHICS, ECONOMICS AND JUSTICE

Rowan Williams

&

Larry Elliott
Economics Editor, Guardian

palgrave
macmillan

Chapter 8, 'Reconciling the Market with the Environment' is adapted from *The Constant Economy: How to Build a Stable Society: How to Create a Stable Society* by Zac Goldsmith, published by Atlantic Books in 2009. Reproduced with permission. Extract from *Red Tory* by Phillip Blond reproduced by permission of Faber and Faber Ltd.

First published 2010 by
PALGRAVE MACMILLAN

Palgrave Macmillan in the UK is an imprint of Macmillan Publishers Limited, registered in England, company number 785998, of Houndmills, Basingstoke, Hampshire RG21 6XS.

Palgrave Macmillan in the US is a division of St Martin's Press LLC, 175 Fifth Avenue, New York, NY 10010.

Palgrave Macmillan is the global academic imprint of the above companies and has companies and representatives throughout the world.

Palgrave® and Macmillan® are registered trademarks in the United States, the United Kingdom, Europe and other countries.

ISBN 978–0–230–25214–1

This book is printed on paper suitable for recycling and made from fully managed and sustained forest sources. Logging, pulping and manufacturing processes are expected to conform to the environmental regulations of the country of origin.

A catalogue record for this book is available from the British Library.

A catalog record for this book is available from the Library of Congress.

10 9 8 7 6 5 4 3 2 1
19 18 17 16 15 14 13 12 11 10

Printed and bound in Great Britain by
CPI Antony Rowe, Chippenham and Eastbourne

CONTENTS

CONTENTS

NOTES ON CONTRIBUTORS

Rowan Williams has been Archbishop of Canterbury since 2002. He was born in 1950 and brought up in Swansea. From 1986 to 1992 he was Lady Margaret Professor of Divinity at Oxford. He served as Bishop of Monmouth from 1992 and Archbishop of Wales from 2000. Dr Williams is a Fellow of the British Academy and is the author of several books on theology; he is also a frequent broadcaster. He is married to Jane, a writer and teacher, and they have two children.

Larry Elliott has been at *The Guardian* since 1988. He is currently Economics Editor and is also the journalist representative on the Scott Trust, which owns the paper. He is the co-author of three books with Dan Atkinson – *The Age of Insecurity* (1998), *Fantasy Island* (2007), warning that Britain's growth under New Labour was a debt-driven illusion, and *The Gods that Failed* (2008), an analysis of the events and forces that brought the global financial system to the brink of collapse. His areas of speciality are the UK and global economy, trade and development. He was part of the group that put together the proposal for a Green New Deal, published by the New Economics Foundation in 2008. Larry is a visiting fellow at Hertfordshire University, a council member of the Overseas Development Institute, an adviser to the Catalyst think tank and to *Red Pepper* magazine, and a magistrate.

Robert Skidelsky is Emeritus Professor of Political Economy at the University of Warwick. His biography of the economist John Maynard Keynes received numerous prizes, including the Lionel Gelber Prize for International Relations and the Council on Foreign Relations Prize for International Relations. He was made a life peer in 1991, and was elected Fellow of the British Academy in 1994. He is the author of *The World After Communism*, and his most recent book, *Keynes: The Return of the Master*, was published in 2009.

Jon Cruddas is MP for Dagenham and Rainham. An MP since 2001, he previously worked as Deputy Political Secretary to Prime Minister Tony Blair, liaising between government and the trade unions.

Jonathan Rutherford is Professor of Cultural Studies at Middlesex University and Editor of the journal *Soundings*. He is also coordinator of the New Political Economy Network. His most recent book is *After Identity* (2007). He has co-edited a number of e-books with Jon Cruddas – *Is the Future Conservative?* (2008) and *The Crash: A View from the Left* (2009), available to download from www.soundings.org.uk.

Phillip Blond is Director of ResPublica, and a research fellow at NESTA (National Endowment for Science, Technology and the Arts). His most recent book, *Red Tory*, was published in 2010.

Adam Lent is Head of the Department of Economic and Social Affairs at the TUC. Previously he was Research Director of the Power Inquiry into political participation in the UK.

John Reynolds originally graduated in theology, but has since had a career as an investment banker, with a particular interest in the energy sector. In addition, since 2006, he has been Chairman of the Church of England Ethical Investment Advisory Group.

Andrew Whittaker is General Counsel to the board at the Financial Services Authority. He is also a non-executive member of the Legal Services Board.

Zac Goldsmith is MP for Richmond Park. He has been Editor of the *Ecologist* magazine since 1997. He is also the author of *The Constant Economy: How to Create a Stable Society* (2009).

Will Hutton is Executive Vice Chair of The Work Foundation. A highly influential commentator on economic issues, he is the author of a number of books, including *The State We're In*. His new book, *Them and Us*, is published in autumn 2010.

FOREWORD

The authors of these essays come from widely differing backgrounds and write from a variety of commitments and convictions. But it is not fanciful to say that there is behind all these pieces a seriousness that can be called both moral and religious – religious in the sense (at the very least) of reverence for the depth and resourcefulness of the human spirit and for the delight and strangeness of the material environment in which we live. As more and more thinkers of our day acknowledge, we shall need all the imaginative resources we can muster to push back at the miserable legacy of a generation of policies and assumptions in much of our public and financial life that can only be called inhuman.

Now that it looks less probable that we are immediately facing a global financial meltdown or even a 1920s-style depression, the temptation is to drift towards the default setting of modern liberal capitalism once more. The point of this book is to insist that this would be monumentally irresponsible; as immoral as it is unintelligent.

The essays collected here focus generally on two kinds of argument. One is a more obviously economic one, and its burden is to challenge the fiction that deregulated globalized capitalism of the variety so aggressively promoted in the 1980s and afterwards was ever a vehicle for sustainable prosperity in sophisticated and flexible economies, let alone for equitable access to wealth and security for the majority of the world's population. A steady theme within that argument is that Keynesian principles have a superior track record in this respect. We therefore would have to ask what there is in the legacy of Keynes's vision of an economics not dictated by uncritical "liberalism" which might need to be recovered and reinstated as a foundation for something that looks a bit more like "common wealth" in our world.

But the second argument is deeper still. The economic ills of the last couple of years have brought to light a widespread anxiety about the kind of society we have become and, even more, the kind of human person, the kind of human consciousness or sensibility we have been encouraging. More and more people have recognized a sickness or deficit in our imagination. There has been an increasing recognition of the ways in which trust and the habits and disciplines of personal exchange and relation have been swept aside in the rush towards profit. We have been rewarding behaviors that are destructive and corrosive of a humane culture. And, as some of these essays point out with varying degrees of intensity, this has impacted on our understanding of the state as well as the individual. Not for nothing does one of our contributors revive the rhetoric of an earlier age in speaking of "the servile state" – an administration unduly obsessed with regulation and control because it has lost the art of educating critical and independent citizens.

In trivializing the meaning of wealth, we have also reduced the range of human reflection and questioning around wellbeing and the good life. And we have done this at a time when – as another of our contributors makes very plain – we need to be asking hard questions about whether our planet can tolerate us as inhabitants for much longer. In other words, to frame the sorts of challenges that emerge in connection with the recent financial crisis, we must broaden our horizons dramatically. Economics has performed least impressively where it has sealed itself off from external challenge or input. Economists who have recognized the porous boundaries of their discipline have, on the contrary, been repeatedly shown to have been talking about that actual world of human agents which some sorts of classical economic discourse appear to disregard. To take only two examples: the Italian tradition of discussing "civil economy" (the title of an intriguing 2007 book by Luigino Bruni and Stefano Zamagni,[1] building on some little-known aspects of the Italian enlightenment) has helped to shape a vocabulary for bringing together what we want to say about civic goods and economic goods; and the work of the Cambridge economist Partha Dasgupta has underlined the necessity of finding ways of factoring both environmental and social costs into the economic calculation.

In one way, much of this book is about reclaiming economics for the humanities. But that is really to say that we are faced with a considerable challenge about what we think of that very idea of "the humanities". We have learned to tolerate forms of thinking that, because they are essentially reductive, tempt us to imagine that the "real world" is the one of conflict and profit – and that the social imagination, the cultivation of relationship, the transformation of an environment into intelligible and beautiful form is so much decorative blather.

But the fact is that, in our economic life as in other areas of human experience, the attempt to survive in a "real world" of such shrunken proportions leads to a condition of extraordinary unreality. The fetishization of financial instruments, the virtual world of debt trading and paper assets, is a fitting symbol of what this real world came to look like. And the very concrete and specific effects of the economics of recent decades in terms of the degradation of social and family fabric ought to wake us up to the urgent need to get back in touch with what we really are as embodied and social creatures. We are not capable of living in mid-air, depending on our electronic support systems. We are happy *with* one another or not at all, it seems, and happy as physical, interdependent subjects, not as greedy wills battling for psychological advantage.

This book is at one level a modest collection of reflections on the disasters and follies of very recent times; but it is in another way an unashamedly immodest and ambitious plea for a renewal of political culture and social vision, a renewal of civic energy and creativity, in our own country and worldwide. We hope it will prompt others to ask how that necessary renewal can be advanced.

ROWAN WILLIAMS
April 2010

NOTE

1. L. Bruni and S. Zamagni, *Civil Economy*, Oxford, 2007.

ACKNOWLEDGMENTS

A book like this is inevitably the work of many hands, and our thanks go to all those who have contributed to its development, writing and production. We begin by thanking those who participated in the March 2009 discussion at Lambeth Palace for taking the time to focus on the ethical aspects of the financial crisis, even as its economic implications continued to unfold. The germ of an idea that eventually became this book began with the sense that afternoon that the discussion taking place at Lambeth Palace desperately needed to take place in the public square as well. This book is an attempt to honor that impulse by bringing together a group of writers who are diverse in their opinions but are all thought-provoking in the development of their views.

The value of a collection of essays like this rests on the efforts of the writers it brings together. So our thanks go most particularly to the authors of the essays contained herein. They have brought to this project a great breadth of expertise and we are immensely grateful for the time and commitment that has gone into their contributions. We would also like to thank Stephen Rutt, Eleanor Davey Corrigan and their colleagues at Palgrave Macmillan for the focus and encouragement they have brought to all stages of this project.

Rowan Williams
Larry Elliott
April 2010

INTRODUCTION

Larry Elliott

The sun was breaking through the clouds in Washington DC when Franklin Roosevelt gave his inaugural presidential address. It was Saturday 4 March 1933 and the United States had just started the slow ascent from the bottom of the economic abyss to which it had sunk in the three years after the Wall Street Crash of 1929. A 50% drop in industrial production meant that factories lay idle and with a quarter of the working population jobless, the dole queue was a feature of every American city. Nor was the malaise confined to the world's biggest economy; the crisis had put paid to the minority Labour government in Britain 18 months previously, while in Germany, a new chancellor, Adolf Hitler, had been in power for little more than a month. A week earlier fire had destroyed the Reichstag building.

Roosevelt said America was facing not just an economic but a moral crisis, and he provided an almost biblical damnation of the excesses that had seen the stock market rise to heady heights in the boom years of the late 1920s. "Practices of the unscrupulous money changers stand indicted in the court of public opinion," the new president said, "rejected by the hearts and minds of men."

Although he did not say as much, Roosevelt clearly hankered for a return to the traditional values – hard work, just reward, respect for others – that Americans believed were exemplified by the Founding Fathers. This moral code had been broken in the Roaring Twenties, when the US had succumbed to "the rules of a generation of self-seekers" and was still, in the president's view, suffering the consequences more than three years after the Wall Street Crash brought the mania in the stock market to an abrupt halt:

> *They have no vision, and when there is no vision the people perish. The money changers have fled from their high seats in the temple of our civilization. We may now restore that temple to the ancient truths. The measure of the restoration lies in the extent to which we apply social values more noble than mere monetary profit.*

Nor was Roosevelt dressing up some modest, technocratic changes to the US economy in flowery language. There were attempts to reflate the economy and attempts to create jobs through public works schemes, and economists have debated their merits ever since. Yet the New Deal was about more than demand management or deficit finance; at root, it was about imposing boundaries on those Wall Street traders who had shown themselves incapable of self-restraint; it was about sharing the spoils of growth more fairly; and, above all, it was about rethinking the market from first principles:

> *Happiness lies not in the mere possession of money; it lies in the joy of achievement, in the thrill of creative effort. The joy and moral stimulation of work no longer must be forgotten in the mad chase of evanescent profits.*

Almost 77 years later, another president found an echo of the Roosevelt era when he outlined plans to reform Wall Street following another profound shock to the financial system. It took a year after his inaugural address, at a White House press conference on 21 January 2010, for Barack Obama to thunder out his words of condemnation, but, even though it was clear that the political impetus had come from the loss to the Democrats of a safe Senate seat in Massachusetts, the spirit of the New Deal was rekindled:

This economic crisis began as a financial crisis, when banks and financial institutions took huge, reckless risks in pursuit of quick profits and massive bonuses. When the dust settled, and this binge of irresponsibility was over, several of the world's oldest and largest financial institutions had collapsed, or were on the verge of doing so. Markets plummeted, credit dried up, and jobs were vanishing by the hundreds of thousands each month. We were on the precipice of a second Great Depression.

The near-death experience of the global economy during the period of financial instability that began in the summer of 2007 is the theme of this book. Like Roosevelt in the 1930s, the authors believe a fundamental rethink is needed, not just to prevent a future financial crisis, but also to counter the threat of climate change, to divide the economic spoils more equitably, and to provide an alternative set of values. A second Great Depression was only averted – if indeed it has been averted – by repudiating the orthodoxy of the previous three decades. Interest rates were cut, banks were bailed out with taxpayers' money, budget deficits allowed to balloon, and printing presses cranked up. The response to the deepest and most widespread downturn since the Second World War was unprecedented action by governments, coordinated worldwide. Although the crisis at first appeared to be merely a local problem in a segment of the American mortgage market, the malaise went far deeper than that; it was also a crisis of economic and political thought, of ideology, of belief and of morality. As in the 1930s, there was a systemic failure that makes the return of "business as usual" untenable and it is this systemic failure that the essays collected in this book try to address.

Since financial markets froze up in early August 2007, there has been a plethora of books detailing each twist and turn in events. Such a panoramic view is beyond the scope of this work, but a brief summary is required. The collapse of communism between 1989 and 1991 brought about deep structural change in the economy, with the reach of the market extended not just to the countries of the former Soviet Union but to the world's two most populous countries – China and India – and to other parts of the developing world. Finance was in the vanguard of what became known as "globalization", with a combination of free movement of capital and developments in digital technology creating a far more integrated market.

Where finance led, manufacturing followed. Cheap labor costs in the developing world meant that companies in the West could "outsource" production, boosting profits and providing cheaper goods for their domestic consumers while limiting the ability of workers in the West to push up wages. The shift in industrial output from West to East led to the build-up of big imbalances in the global economy, between those countries running big balance of trade surpluses and those running big deficits. Surplus countries were neither exclusively Asian nor exclusively poor; Japan and Germany both relied heavily on exports for their growth. The US and Britain were the two most important deficit nations, and they were able to use the new system of global finance to live beyond their means for many years. Countries such as China wanted Americans and Britons to carry on buying their exports, so they helped fund the trade deficits in the West by buying up assets, normally in the form of government bonds. The flow of money into Wall Street and the City of London pushed up the value of the dollar and the pound, making imports cheaper and exports dearer. This not only made the imbalances worse, it also resulted in asset price bubbles in America, Britain and some other European countries because cheaper imports resulted in lower levels of inflation, which in turn allowed central banks to cut interest rates.

Traders in the financial markets of London, Tokyo and New York were confident that the money-go-round would never end because it was common knowledge that Alan Greenspan, the chairman of the Federal Reserve, the US central bank, would shore up asset prices if a crash were threatened. This happened in 1998, when Long-Term Capital Management, a hedge fund, was on the point of bankruptcy and again after shares in technology stocks collapsed in the dot-com meltdown of 2000 and 2001. Each time, Greenspan cut interest rates to a lower level and left them there until he was quite sure that the economy was growing strongly once more. Put simply, the problems of one bubble were solved by the creation of another, and this culminated in the biggest boom-bust in the American housing market between 2003 and 2008.

Greenspan's response to the drop in technology stocks and the terrorist attacks in New York and Washington on 11 September 2001 was to cut interest rates to 1%, where he left them for the next two years. The easy availability of cheap credit encouraged Americans to borrow money to buy homes, and the first people attracted into the market were so-called "prime borrowers", those people with good jobs and decent salaries. Prices rose, encouraging construction firms to build more homes that, in turn, required an ever-bigger army of mortgage providers, real estate agents, lawyers and retailers.

Once the prime buyers were exhausted, however, there was a potential problem. The boom could only go on provided house prices continued to go up and that necessitated a steady flow of first-time buyers, this time those without such good prospects. Indeed, the "subprime borrowers" often had very poor prospects indeed; many had low-paid, insecure jobs and often they had no history of employment whatsoever. In a calculated, quite cynical fashion, millions of subprime borrowers were enticed into the US mortgage market with home loans that were affordable in the short run but would become ruinously expensive after two years, when the interest rate on the loan rose sharply. Concerned borrowers were told not to worry; house prices were going up strongly so anybody struggling with their monthly repayments at a later date would be able to sell at a profit.

The mortgage providers knew well that some of those taking out "liar" loans (lying about their employment history or income) or "Ninja" loans (no income, no job or assets) were poor risks but didn't much care. In previous decades, lenders had been more cautious since they held the mortgages on their own books and could suffer a direct financial loss in the event of default. By the mid-2000s, mortgage providers were able to rid themselves of their "toxic waste" (the risky subprime loans) by selling them on to Wall Street banks. The bad loans were then mixed up with good loans in the process known as "securitization", and the resulting securities were then sold in the financial markets. Highly complex mathematical models of the economy were developed to assess the risk of these derivative products, and the conclusion was that while the risk was very low indeed, the rewards were considerable. Financial institutions, both in the US and Asia, found the attraction of easy money too tempting to resist, and invested heavily in subprime debt.

All of which was fine while house prices continued to rise. But by late 2006, the market had reached saturation point. Interest rates had risen from 1% to 5.25% and there were no more subprime buyers to gull. Prices of real estate fell and for the first time questions were asked about the true value of the complex derivatives that banks had on their balance sheets. The answer was that their market value was a fraction of their ostensible book value, but nobody knew for sure how small that fraction was, nor was it clear just how exposed each bank was.

That was the state of the world in early August 2007. Six weeks earlier, Gordon Brown had used his last big speech as chancellor of the exchequer to deliver a panegyric to big finance, boasting that the City was enjoying a new golden age. On the other side of the Atlantic, Chuck Prince, the chief executive of Citigroup, saw no reason why the hints of trouble in the American housing market should put paid to the boom conditions on Wall Street. In an interview in the *Financial Times* on 7 July 2007, he said:

When the music stops, in terms of liquidity, things will become complicated. But as long as the music is playing, you've got to get up and dance. We're still dancing.

What Prince did not know was that the music he could hear playing was the modern equivalent of the orchestra playing on the *Titanic*. The downturn in the US housing market was not the equivalent of a brief squall on an otherwise placid sea; it was a colossal iceberg.

Historically, economic implosions go through a number of distinct phases, and this one was no exception. First, there is the bubble phase, a long period of growth, often associated with a financial innovation, during which asset prices rise strongly and individuals borrow more. From the tulip mania in Amsterdam of the 1630s to the surge in land prices in Tokyo in the 1980s, the bubbles have always burst, but during this first euphoric phase of the cycle, those with the temerity to point this out are met with the four most dangerous words in financial markets: "It's different this time."

The notion that it is not different this time takes time to sink in, which is why the second phase of the cycle is denial. From August 2007 to March 2008, there was a belief, widely held among policy makers, that the return to business as usual would be swift. The talk was of a soft landing, of a slowdown in growth but no outright recession, and of the decoupling of the high saving Asian economies from the debt-ridden US. By the spring of 2008, when the UK government was forced to nationalize Northern Rock and the US government stepped in to find a buyer for the ailing investment bank, Bear Stearns, the mood turned darker.

The third phase of the cycle – grudging acceptance – lasted from March 2008 until the collapse of Lehman Brothers six months later. With unemployment rising and output falling, there was little choice but to admit that the problems caused by the freezing-up of financial markets was a lot more serious than at first thought. Even so, the assumption was that the effects of the credit crunch would be shallow and that recovery would be rapid. Alistair Darling, delivering his first budget speech as chancellor of the exchequer in March 2008, exemplified the mood when he boasted that the UK was "better placed than other economies to withstand the downturn in the global economy". Growth in 2009, according to the UK Treasury, would be between 2.25% and 2.75%; the actual outcome was markedly worse, with output falling by 5% in the biggest one-year decline since 1921.

Everything changed on 15 September 2008, when the US Treasury admitted it could not find a buyer for Lehman Brothers, one of America's oldest investment banks. At that moment, the last vestiges of denial were stripped away and grudging acceptance gave way to phase four of the cycle – panic. For the next four weeks, no bank, no matter how big or prestigious, was considered entirely safe. Share prices fell, the price of credit – on the rare occasions it was obtainable – became prohibitively expensive. The banks, which for the past two decades had been pillorying governments, urging the state to "get out of the way" of the wealth creators in the private sector, now begged for help. Bailouts were duly organized, but the winter of 2008–09 saw global industrial production and world trade contract at rates equivalent to those of the early 1930s. Governments responded by turning to the remedies proposed by John Maynard Keynes three-quarters of a century earlier; they cut interest rates to barely above zero; they boosted government spending; and they created new electronic money through a process known as "quantitative easing". Robert Lucas, a Nobel Prize-winning alumnus of the Chicago School, summed up the intellectual bankruptcy of neoliberal economists when he noted ruefully: "We are all Keynesians in a foxhole."[1]

The final phase of the cycle is in some ways the most important. Once the immediate panic is over, as it was by the spring of 2009, when it became apparent that governments had saved the banking system from collapse, the question was what sort of reforms would be necessary to ensure that the breathing space led to a lasting recovery rather than a brief interlude before a relapse. As stock markets rallied and growth rates bottomed out, one theory was that capitalism was once again demonstrating its remarkable resilience and that only modest changes to regulation and supervision would be needed to prevent the irrational exuberance of financial markets leading to a future crisis.

That, to the authors of this volume, is a perverse reading of events. There is no more chance of "business as usual" than there was of the war that started in August 1914 being "all over by Christmas". The long boom of the 1990s and early 2000s has been an Edwardian summer in which America has replaced Britain as the superpower whose hegemony is under threat, the wars in Iraq and Afghanistan are the modern equivalent of the Boer War, and the Marines are the Royal Navy a century on. The outbreak of the First World War was the start of a profound upheaval that witnessed the bloodiest conflict in the history of mankind, the deepest depression since the advent of modern industrial capitalism and the rise of totalitarian governments. Ultimately, this upheaval led to policies designed to tame the excesses of financial capital, to ensure that the fruits of growth were shared more equitably, and to put in place international institutions designed to create the conditions for peace and prosperity. At a domestic level, welfare states, full employment policies and curbs on the activities of capital were a response to the mass unemployment and inequality of the interwar era. The United Nations, the World Bank and the International Monetary Fund were their equivalent at a global level.

This postwar settlement was never accepted by economic liberals; indeed, the reforms were seen as an intolerable interference in the workings of the free market. The liberal fightback started almost as soon as the Second World War ended, but only gained traction in the 1970s when the full employment welfare model of Keynes and Beveridge struggled to cope with the inflation caused by the cost of the Vietnam War and the fivefold increase in oil prices.

The combination of lower growth and higher inflation – or "stagflation" as it became known – gave rise to a new form of political economy, based on a different set of principles. Markets, particularly capital markets, were to be freed from restrictions; the bargaining power of labor was to be broken; state-owned monopolies were to be sold off; competition was to be injected into monopolies; taxes were to be cut to stimulate enterprise; and welfare states were to be pared back. These ideological changes meshed with changes in the way the world worked. A communications revolution was transforming the speed at which transactions could take place, giving the "global herd" the opportunity to provide instant judgment on decisions made by governments. In the West, manufacturing lost its dominance to a growing financial sector, which in countries such as the US and Britain accounted for an ever-bigger share of national output. The spread of the global market accelerated with the end of the Cold War.

It was assumed by supporters of this "new world order" – who tended to be the rich and the powerful – that these reforms and structural changes would combine to make for a more prosperous and stable global economy. This proved not to be the case. Growth rates were lower and unemployment rates higher than in the Keynesian decades immediately after the Second World War; financial crises, notable by their absence from 1945 to 1970, began to reappear once the controls on capital were relaxed.

The late American economist Hyman Minsky said this phenomenon was easy to explain. Those working in deregulated financial markets started off with a cautious approach, but as time went by they became more and more willing to take risks. The subprime mortgage scandal exposed six unattractive, not to say dangerous, features of global finance: there was a surfeit of speculation in what the chairman of the UK Financial Services Authority, Lord Adair Turner, called "socially useless" activities; there was a recklessness caused by a belief that dealers had a fail-safe model; there was too much greed; there was a supreme arrogance that the rewards being made were justified rather than being the profits of a bubble; there was rule by oligarchy, with the financial sector expecting tame politicians to listen to the power of money; and there was a corrosive belief that there was no such thing as excess.

It was, by early 2007, a highly combustible mixture. The global economy was divided between the spenders and the savers. Domestic economies in the spendthrift nations were heavily reliant on debt and rising asset prices. Britain, for example, was an economy kept aloft by three engines of growth; the City of London, the housing market and public spending. Excess profits from asset bubbles in the first two sectors helped provide the tax revenues for investment in the third. But not only were Britain and the US highly unbalanced, they were also highly unequal. The gap between rich and poor had widened sharply; pay at the top had risen, while pay for those in the middle and at the bottom had stagnated. Interestingly, globalization was cited as the reason why salaries had to go up for executives (the need to tap into a pool of highly sought-after talent) and why pay had to be held down for those at the bottom (the competition from cheap labor in the developing world).

This was a world where the financial sector ruled supreme. It was responsible for the huge financial flows in and out of economies, and for the high levels of leverage that amplified the profits when the gambles turned out to be right and magnified the losses when they went wrong. On the eve of the crisis, it was as if the designers of a Formula One racing car had souped up the engine, removed the brakes, put a boy racer behind the wheel on a street crowded with pedestrians, and invited him to put his foot down. It was an accident waiting to happen. When the accident duly occurred, there was initially disbelief, followed by a lengthy period of denial in which it was assumed that the crisis was superficial and would have no long-lasting ill effects. This was, perhaps, understandable, since those who had worked tirelessly to replace the postwar welfare state model with free-market economics had done so because they were convinced that a reliance on the price mechanism rather than collectivism was both economically rational and – by returning power to the individual – morally stronger. That conviction was, if anything, strengthened by the experience of the string of mini-crises that had afflicted the global economy – from the Latin American debt defaults of 1982 to the collapse of the dot-com bubble at the turn of the millennium. Despite sending tremors, often quite severe tremors, through the global economy, none caused permanent damage, or so it seemed.

Yet the stock market crash of 1987, the Asian financial crisis a decade later and the bailout of Long-Term Capital Management were not evidence of resilience but warnings that something was not right with the prevailing economic and financial order. It took a seizure to the global banking system to reveal precisely that that "something" was more than a simple design flaw that could be corrected with a technical fix but stemmed from moral and ethical failings.

To take but one example, a core belief for those who opposed state interference in the economy was that individuals and institutions should "stand on their own two feet" in the way that the pioneers of the Industrial Revolution or the homesteaders of the American West had made their own way in the world. Yet when the global financial system trembled on the brink of systemic collapse in the autumn of 2008, it was to the reviled state that the bankers turned, insisting that their institutions were "too big to fail". The banks, many of which had set up offshore subsidiaries in Jersey or the Cayman Islands to minimize their tax payments, now insisted that taxpayers should bail them out. Not content with this, the banks then found out that the money provided by governments to replenish the capital lost in speculative ventures, together with the raft of policies used to reflate economies pushed into deep recession by the financial crisis, allowed them to make large profits from their own trades in the markets. When the public caviled at these windfall profits funding a new round of seven-figure bonuses, the bankers at first failed to see what all the fuss was about and complained bitterly in the UK when the chancellor, Alistair Darling, imposed a windfall levy.

Dhaval Joshi, an economist with RAB Capital in the City, said that by providing such lavish bailouts for their financial sectors, Obama and Brown had presided over the "most unfair recovery in modern economic history", with all the proceeds in the US and 90% of the proceeds in the UK going to extra profits, and little or nothing going to wage earners. Governments had created the perfect environment for banks to make profits: they had recapitalized struggling institutions; they had provided loan guarantees; they had cut interest rates to 0%; and they had been a receptacle for the "toxic assets" that were burdening bank balance sheets. Simultaneously, companies in Britain and the US were laying off staff and imposing pay restraint and short-time working on those who remained. Joshi said:

> *And now comes insult to add to injury. Having exclusively boosted current corporate profits, the stimulus will almost certainly be paid for from future wages. Because if policymakers do tackle the huge deficits that have funded the stimulus, it inevitably means public sector jobs cuts combined with tax rises.[2]*

This, though, had been the pattern for the entire crisis. President John F. Kennedy said that, in the postwar US, economic growth was like a rising tide that lifted all boats. That was not the case during the boom-bust of the first decade of the twenty-first century, when the rewards went to those already blessed and the costs fell on those who could ill afford to bear them. In the US, a complex superstructure of collateralized debt obligations, credit default swaps and tranches of securitized loans depended on new buyers willing to keep the housing boom going. At the peak, 250,000 mortgage brokers were criss-crossing the country looking for those they could persuade, cajole or dupe into taking out loans they could not afford. "Why would any sane person lend money to someone with no income, job or assets", said one commentator on the crisis. "Answer: because they were selling the loan to somebody else, so they didn't care."[3]

It is the conjecture of this book that we should care if the vulnerable are deliberately preyed upon; we should care if the structure of financial markets provides incentives for short-term enrichment over long-term stability; we should care if the prevailing economic model is at odds with the future of the planet; and we should care if the values that underpin the market are corrosive. When Archbishop Rowan Williams called a meeting to discuss the crisis at Lambeth Palace in March 2009, the economic cycle was at its nadir; factories had been mothballed, ships lay idle at port, unemployment was rising rapidly and bank credit had been reduced to a trickle. Not all those who were present that day have been able to contribute to this book, but the spirit of that sunny spring afternoon has been captured.

Like that gathering, this volume is an ecumenical affair, spanning left and right, market insiders, environmentalists, regulators, trade unionists, politicians and academics. Here we have Lord Robert Skidelsky warning of the perils of forgetting the lessons of John Maynard Keynes and the investment banker John Reynolds stressing the need for a culture change in his industry to reflect ethical values. Zac Goldsmith argues that the future of the planet depends on a reworked market system, while Will Hutton makes the case for fairness. From the left, Jon Cruddas and Jonathan Rutherford call for a new political economy based on a long tradition of political economy, while from the right, Phillip Blond attacks market fundamentalism. Adam Lent says that the new economics of diversity requires a supportive state, while Andrew Whittaker tackles the case for tougher financial regulation. Rowan Williams recognizes the importance of economics, but stresses that economics is not everything, and that there will be no sustainable human society until its limitations are recognized.

This is the key message of this book. None of the authors in this book believe it is possible to turn the clock back to a prelapsarian golden age, real or imagined; instead, they want the financial markets to be put back in their proper place. The crisis that began in August 2007 has been the catalyst for new thinking at the highest levels of policy-making. Mervyn King, the governor of the Bank of England, has seen merit in separating retail banking from investment banking, one of the key reforms introduced by Roosevelt in the 1930s and a feature of the US financial system until the late 1990s. Adair Turner has made the case for a financial transaction tax, an idea first floated by the American economist James Tobin in the early 1970s. The notion that financial instability, climate change and the depletion of fossil fuels form a "triple crunch" has given risen to calls for a Green New Deal, in which investment from more tightly regulated banks is channeled into renewable power, environmental businesses and making homes more energy efficient. Despite the severity of the crisis, resistance to the radical changes needed has been strong, not least because one of the key changes will involve greater humility about what we as humans do and don't know, and humility is a virtue not found in abundance in the global financial markets. The reform process will be long and difficult; the struggle will only be won if victory is first achieved in the battle of ideas. Roosevelt once said:

The fundamental trouble with this whole stock market crowd is their lack of elementary education. I do not mean a lack of college diplomas, and so on, but just inability to understand the country or public or their obligations to their fellow man.

We hope this book contributes, in some small way, to the re-education process.

NOTES

1. Cited by J. Fox in "The comeback Keynes", *Time*, 27 January 2009.
2. D. Joshi, "The unfairest recovery", RAB Capital, March 2010.
3. J. Lanchester, *Whoops!: Why Everyone Owes Everyone and No One Can Pay*, Allen Lane, 2010.

1

KNOWING OUR LIMITS

Rowan Williams

It is quite striking that in the gospel parables Jesus more than once uses the world of economics as a framework for his stories – the parable of the talents, the dishonest steward, even, we might say, the little vignette of the lost coin. Like farming, like family relationships, like the tensions of public political life, economic relations have something to say to us about how we see our humanity in the context of God's action. Money is a metaphor alongside other things; our money transactions, like our family connections and our farming and fishing labors, bring out features of our human condition that, rightly understood, tell us something of how we might see our relation to God and God's to us. A story about how people do and don't take risks with what they have been given or about an eccentric landowner who insists on paying all his employees the same wage, however long or hard they have been working, becomes a window into the strangeness of God – like the stories about broken families, careless farmers sowing seed all over the place or unwelcome and disgusting foreigners offering life-saving compassion when the usual neighbors are nowhere to be seen.

The point doesn't need to be labored. Monetary exchange is simply one of the things people do. It can be carried out well or badly, honestly or dishonestly, generously or meanly. It is one of those areas of life in which our decisions show who we are, and so it is a proper kind of raw material for stories designed to suggest how encounter with God shows us who we are. All obvious enough, you may think. But we should reflect further on this – because we have become used in our culture to an attitude to economics which more or less turns the parables on their head. In this new framework, economic motivations, relationships, conventions and so on are the fundamental thing and the rest is window-dressing. Instead of economics being one source of metaphor among others for the realities of self-definition and self-discovery, other ways of speaking and understanding are substitutes for economic assessment. The language of customer and provider has wormed its way into practically all areas of our social life, even education and healthcare, and we forget that it is a *metaphor* when we call a student, a patient or a traveler a "customer". The implication is that the most basic relation between one human being and another or one group and another is that of the carefully calibrated exchange of material resources; the most basic kind of assessment we can make about the actions of another, from the trader to the nurse to the politician, is the evaluation of how much they can increase my liberty to negotiate favorable deals and maximize my resources.

In asking whether economics and theology represent two different worlds, we need to be aware of the fact that a lot of contemporary economic language and habit doesn't only claim a privileged status for economics on the grounds that it works by innate laws to which other considerations are irrelevant. It threatens to reduce other sorts of discourse to its own terms – to make a bid for one world in which everything reduces to one set of questions. If we want to challenge the idea that theology and economics do belong in completely separate frames, the first thing we need to do, paradoxically, is to hang on to the idea that there really *are* different ways of talking about human activity and that not everything reduces to one sovereign model or standard of value. Economic exchange is *one of the things people do*. Treat it as the only "real" thing people do and you face the same problems that face the evolutionary biologist for whom the only question is how organisms compete and survive, or the fundamentalist Freudian for whom the only issue is how we resolve the tensions of infantile sexuality.

In each of these reductive contexts, there is something of the same process going on. Each will tell you that your capacity to examine yourself and clarify for yourself who you are in the light of your memory and your imagination, your language and your variegated relationships is a fiction – or at best a small and insignificant aspect of your identity. The face you see in the mirror is not the real thing: you are being activated by hidden motives and calculations, you are unconsciously balancing out the forces that are involved in guaranteeing your chances of survival as a carrier of genetic material or in mediating and controlling the frustrations of Oedipal desire – or in securing the maximal control of disposable resources in a world of scarcity and competition. All these models leave you with an uncomfortable lack of clarity about whether you can really take intelligent decisions at all on the basis of the kind of person you consciously want to be. They all tell you that you are carrying an agenda you have not determined, that you are in some way being used by large and impersonal powers.

It is too easy to claim that the theological or ethical perspective simply restores some kind of innocence to these decisions, so that we do not have to worry about the economic or psychoanalytic versions of human agency. Traditional religious ethics – in fact, traditional ethics of any kind – does not require you to ignore the hidden forces that may be at work in any particular setting, and it does not offer an account of human action that leaves out these ambiguous readings and possibilities. But it does claim that being aware of them is no more than a part of something else. The "larger" picture is not the one that economics or biology or psychodynamics dictates. It is the richly textured process of shaping a story that is your own. The questions about what in fact flows in to this or that action, all the obscure and often unwelcome factors that make us constantly less free than we fantasize we ought to be, are taken up in a *strategy of integration* – a habit of picturing yourself as a single self-continuous agent who can make something distinctive out of all this material. Being a human self is learning how to ask critical questions of your own habits and compulsions, your own shadowed and many layered motivation, so as to adjust how you act in the light of a model of human behavior, both individual and collective, that represents some fundamental truth about what humanity is *for*. Put like this, it is possible to see the various balancing acts we engage in, the calculations of self-interest and security, the resolution of buried tensions, as aspects of finding our way to a life that *manifests* something – instead of just solving this or that problem of survival or profit. It is really to claim that our job as human beings is to *imagine ourselves*, using all the raw material that science or psychoanalysis or economics can generate for us, but not treating any of this as completely determinative – in the hope that the images we shape or discover will have resonance and harmony with the rhythms of how things most deeply are in the universe, with what Christians and others call the will and purpose of Almighty God. We shall be coming back to some of the detail of this later on.

If all that is clear to begin with, we can also begin to see economics in its proper place. It is one thing that people do, yes; but perhaps at this stage of the argument we can grant that it has a very special importance. In the past few years, I have found myself repeatedly noting that the term "economy" itself is in its origins simply the word for "housekeeping". And if this is the root or the core of its sense, we ought to be able to learn something about where the whole discourse belongs by thinking through what housekeeping actually is. A household is somewhere where life is lived in common; and housekeeping is guaranteeing that this common life has some stability about it that allows the members of the household to grow and flourish and act in useful ways. A working household is an environment in which vulnerable people are nurtured and allowed to grow up (children) or wind down (the elderly); it is a background against which active people can go out to labor in various ways to reinforce the security of the household; it is a setting where leisure and creativity can find room in the general business of intensifying and strengthening the relationships that are involved.

Good housekeeping seeks common wellbeing so that all these things can happen; and we should note that the one thing required in a background of wellbeing is stability – the kind of stability that allows a margin of generous welcome to those who are not currently contributing to the material resources of the household, and allows all the inhabitants of the household to have some space for "nonproductive" living. Housekeeping theory is about how we use our intelligence to balance the needs of all those involved and to secure trust between them. A theory that wanders too far from these basics is a recipe for damage to the vulnerable, to the regularity and usefulness of labor and to the possibilities human beings have for renewing (and challenging) themselves through leisure and creativity.

This is the kind of damage that manifestly results from an economic climate in which everything reduces to the search for maximized profit and unlimited material growth. The effects of trying to structure economic life independently of intelligent choice about long-term goals for human beings have become more than usually visible in the past 18 months: it is harder than it was to ignore the force of the question, "what for?" in thinking about the global market. What is the long-term wellbeing we seek? What is the human face we want to see, in the mirror and in our neighbors? Have we really created a "household" in which there is security for those who cannot defend themselves? The isolated *homo economicus* of the old textbooks, making rational calculations of self-interest, has been exposed as a straw man: the search for profit at a fantastic cost in terms of risk and unrealism has shown that there can be a form of economic "rationality" that is in fact wildly irrational. And, over the past two or three decades, the impact of a narrow economic rationality on public services in our society has shown how there can be a "housekeeping" strategy that ends up destroying the nurture and stability that make a household what it is. What we most need, it seems, is to recover that vision of what the Chief Rabbi in the UK has called "the home we build together".[1]

So the question of how we think about shared wellbeing is the central one before us. If we are not to be reduced to speaking about this only in vague terms of the control of material resources, we need a language that allows us to imagine and to criticize our humanity in relation to something more than the immediate environment.

Theology does not solve specific economic questions (any more than it solves specific political or scientific ones); but what it offers is a robust definition of what human wellbeing looks like and what the rationale is for human life well lived in common.

Central to what Christian theology sets before us is mutuality. The Christian Scriptures describe the union of those who are identified with Jesus Christ as having an organic quality, a common identity shaped by the fact that each depends on all others for their life. This is St Paul's argument in the twelfth chapter of his First Letter to the Corinthians. No element in the Body is dispensable or superfluous: what affects one affects all, for good and ill, since both suffering and flourishing belong to the entire organism not to any individual or purely local grouping. The model of human existence that is taken for granted is one in which each person is both needy and needed, both dependent on others and endowed with gifts for others. And while this is not presented in terms of what we might think of as a general social program, it is manifestly what the biblical writers see as the optimal shape of human life, life in which the purposes of God are made plain. Jesus' own teaching and practice make it quite explicit that the renewed people of God cannot exist when certain categories are systematically excluded, so that the wholeness of the community requires them to be invited. St Paul spells out the implications in terms of the metaphor of organic unity in the Body; St John recalls the teaching of Jesus at the Last Supper about the divine purpose which is to create a oneness among human beings that will mirror the oneness of Jesus and the eternal source of his being. "Indwelling" in one another is the ground of Christian ethics. Each believer is called to see himself or herself as equally helpless alone and gifted in relationship.

Helpless alone and gifted in relationship: this is where we start in addressing the world of economics from a Christian standpoint – and the work of Jonathan Sacks, already referred to, should remind us that it has important analogues in the Jewish context. Sacks speaks of the close connection between giving and belonging,[2] in a way that echoes the emphasis here on justice as involving making people capable of *giving* into the common life. No process whose focus is the limited or exclusive security of an individual or an interest group or even national community alone can be regarded as unequivocally good in Jewish and Christian terms, because of the underlying aspiration to a state of security in isolation which it reveals. If my wellbeing is inseparable in God's community from the wellbeing of all others, a global economic ethic in which the indefinitely continuing poverty or disadvantage of some is taken for granted has to be decisively left behind. This is not only about conscious intentions – not all that many people would deliberately articulate their economic goals in terms of excluding others. But it is the taking for granted that is most problematic; we stop noticing that the effect of certain economic habits is *in fact* exclusion, and we stand in constant need of awakening to the long-reach consequences of what we have assumed, whether at the local and national level or in the international markets. And the ethical point in this, remember, is not simply that there is an imperative to be generous to others but that there is an imperative to recognize our own need and dependence even on those who appear to have nothing to give. To separate our destiny from that of the poor of the world, or from the rejected or disabled in our own context, is to compromise that destiny and to invite a life that is less than whole for ourselves.

To use a different but perhaps helpful metaphor, our life together reflects the way our very language works. We speak because we are spoken to and learn to become partakers in human conversation by being invited into a flow of verbal life that has already begun. It is simply and literally impossible for us to learn and use language without acknowledging dependence; aspirations to an isolated life in this context are straightforwardly meaningless. No word or phrase is simply a possession; it is there to pass on, to use in the creation of a shared reality. And the worst abuses and misconceptions of language are those in which words and phrases are "traded" (an interesting metaphor in this connection!) in ways that do not seek to build that shared reality – whether this is a matter of using language as a weapon or using it as a way of concealing truth or using it to manipulate judgment and desire. It is not an accident that in a context where injustice and narrow judgment prevail in economic relations, language itself becomes stale or dead. If we think of how much "dead" language there is around in our culture – in bad journalistic writing, in advertising, in propaganda, in official jargon – we may get a clear glimpse of just how bad our economic life has become. We talk, in another powerful and significant financial metaphor, of "debasing the currency" of our speech. We know that it is possible for us to forget that we need *living* language – honest language, fresh metaphors, new puzzles and challenges – for our life to be as it should. We depend on others generating this living speech and we need to be able ourselves to contribute to it: the silence of cliché and cynicism is the diabolical mirror image of the silence that comes on the far side of the most creative speech. The silence of cliché is what happens when there seems no point in listening for the new, and no energy for active response to what is said. You might as well say x as say y: everything is exchangeable. Which is itself a characteristic of the market mentality: everything can be measured and thus replaced by something of equivalent significance as far as material profit and security are concerned. Paying the right kind of attention to the corruptions of language in our age is inseparable from attending to the corruptions of our economic exchanges; and it is no less of a religious obligation.

In sum, faith educates us at the same time in dependence and in the authority of the giver; and in our current climate, this particular balance is one of the hardest to achieve. But if our economic life is indeed "one of the things we do", it will be marked in its actual operations by just the same constraints and buried rhythms or tensions that appear in other aspects of what we do. To the extent that theology has something to say about those rhythms and tensions, it has something to say to economics.

If what we have said so far makes sense, theology contributes two things to the discussion of an ethical economic future. It challenges, as we have seen, the idea that there is a mysterious uniqueness about economic life that takes it out of the normal scope of our discussions of intelligent choice and the humane evaluation of options. It proposes a model of human life together that insists on the fact that we are all involved in the fate of any individual or group and that no one is either exempt from damage or incapable of gift within the human community as God intends it. But the second aspect worth noting – to pick up from an earlier part of this discussion – is that, by underlining the fact that we do have the capacity for truthful self-understanding and thus for intelligent scrutiny of alternative courses of action, the Christian theological vision also offers a critical account of what human *personality* can be. It provides a basis for talking about character and thus about virtue (as I have suggested elsewhere). It takes for granted that we have a proper interest in the continuity, the intelligibility, of our lives; that we have a proper interest, to use a slightly different idiom, in integrity – in being recognizable to ourselves from moment to moment and being answerable for ourselves from moment to moment. It is clear enough, alas, that regulation alone is ill equipped to solve our problems: the issues need to be internalized in terms of the sort of life that humans might find actively desirable and admirable, the sort of biographies that carry conviction by their self-consistency. And this means recovering the language of the virtues and the courage to speak of what a good life looks like – as well as the clarity to identify what has gone wrong in our society when we fail to set out a clear picture of the good life as it appears in trade and finance as much as in the classical professions.

Classically, the "cardinal" virtues of fortitude, prudence, temperance and justice propose a picture of human excellence – or, from another point of view, human ordinariness – characterized by a lack of self-protective anxiety, by realism about the possible effects of actions, by self-awareness and self-control in managing our appetites, our lust and acquisitiveness, and by a clear conviction that the same respect and serious attention is owed to all our fellow humans so that we act not only with abstract fairness but with care towards all. All of them presuppose – though we may not at first notice this – a certain attitude to *time,* an attitude which does not see time as always scarce and pressured. These are human skills we need to learn; virtue is something to do with the long view and with a concerted resistance to superficiality. Richard Sennett, in his book *The Craftsman*, describes eloquently the ways in which the culture of modern capitalism privileges ways of working in which there is no space for the reflection that may lead to intuitive freshness, asking new questions, or for depth of absorption in skills: "the craftsman's ability to dig deep" is sidelined, and the effect is feverish and shallow management of problems.[3] As he has argued in other works like *The Culture of the New Capitalism*,[4] the very idea of good work is weakened by an approach to profit-making which ignores the need in human beings to *grow*, to develop an identity over time that has continuity and three-dimensionality. The skills of good work are deeply connected with the skills of "inhabiting" our world as it actually is, and thus with virtue – with taking time to be at home with self and environment in the ways that are least damaging and most creative for all who share the same human space.

Christianity of course supplemented the cardinal virtues with the "theological" virtues of faith, hope and love, asserting that the free, reasonable, self-aware person formed in the cardinal virtues would need a rootedness in trustful relationship with God that could "anchor" the vulnerable self in a relation which could not be destroyed by success or failure in the world's terms. But whether or not this ultimate anchorage is there, the virtuous life still stands as a model of inhabiting the world in a way that seeks not to damage or to control or to avoid cost, but to live what some would call an "adult" human life – though in fact we can learn quite a lot about it from children and from others who (to refer back to what was said earlier) do not have to justify themselves in the world of competitive production. We urgently need to dust off this language of virtue and to try and understand why it has come to be that we have left ourselves so generally deprived of "models for inhabiting the world".

This means in turn rescuing the concept of civic virtue and connecting it with individual moral wellbeing; which involves reclaiming the idea that public life is a possible vocation for the morally serious person. The discussion we have embarked on here is not simply about the theological grounds for a more just social order, although it is at least that; it is also a matter of grasping that "wellbeing" involves the capacity, in the words that some contemporary philosophers like to use, of bearing one's own scrutiny – being able to look at yourself without despair or contempt. This is not at all the same as looking at yourself with complacency or self-congratulation. It is to do with developing a discerning self-awareness that is awake to possible corruptions, able to ask questions of all sorts of emotional and self-directed impulses, and capable of developing habits of honest self-examination. It depends not on the confidence of getting or having got things right but on the confidence that it is possible steadily to expose yourself to the truth, whatever your repeated failures to live in and through it. Wellbeing entails a dimension of hopeful honesty which keeps alive the conviction that learning and change are real in human life and that there can be a story to be told that will hold a life together with some sort of coherence. And, so the claim goes, if this can be nurtured and maintained, it is the necessary condition for any public involvement that does not collapse into managerial efforts to balance warring group interests. Personal virtue liberates people for civic virtue. Not that "virtuous" civic life thereby becomes easy or its choices obvious and uncontroversial; but critical and self-critical imagination is acknowledged as an essential aspect of the political enterprise.

The contribution of theology to economic decision-making is not only about raising questions concerning the common good, questions to do with how this or that policy grants or withholds liberty for the most disadvantaged. These are obviously necessary matters, and a sound theological stress on mutuality, on the balance of dependence and gift sketched earlier, is crucial to our public discussion of economics. But we need also to look with the greatest of care at what is being assumed and what is being actively promoted by our economic practices about human motivation, about character and integrity. This impacts of course on the integrity of business practice; but it also has to do with assumptions about competition, about the priority of work over family, about what advertising appeals to and what behavior is rewarded. If we find, as a good many commentators and researchers have observed in recent years, that working practices regularly reward behavior that is undermining of family life, driven or obsessional, relentlessly competitive and adversarial, we have some questions to ask. As well as working for a global economic order that is just and mutual, we need habits in the actual workings of the financial "industry" that do not destroy what I called earlier "discerning self-awareness" and the capacity for humane relationships. If the nourishing of personal virtue is one of the things that enables a different kind of politics, then in turn political and macroeconomic decisions should have in view the degree to which they either support or undermine the possibilities of virtuous life for particular persons and their families and small-scale communities.

Economic activity is something people do, one kind of activity among others, and as such, it is subject to the same moral considerations as all other activities. It has to be thought about in connection with what we actively want for our humanity. And questions about what we want will take us beyond "pure" economic categories, just as surely as talking seriously about politics or technology will take us outside a narrowly specialized discourse once we want to know what they're for. Human life is indeed a tapestry of diverse activities, not reducible to each other. It is not the case that all motivation is "really" economic, that all relations are actually to do with exchange and the search for profit. Yet it can be said with some reason that economics in the sense of housekeeping is a background for other things; and because of that it is particularly important to keep an eye on its moral contours. Get this wrong and many other things go wrong, in respect of individual character as well as social relations.

Thus we are bound to look for the sort of language that will keep our imagination and our critical faculties alive in this enterprise, that will keep us alert to the dangers of all sorts of reductionism. Theology in one way does represent a "separate" frame of reference, one that doesn't at all depend on how things turn out in this world for its system of values. That's why it is not in competition with other sorts of discourse. It would be a serious mistake to claim that there were exhaustive theological "explanations" for this or that piece of behavior which could not be true if you accepted psychological or economic or neurological accounts. Yet equally theological descriptions of human behavior are not simply an optional gloss on the iron world of fact. They describe behavior in relation to the agency on which everything depends, the intelligent love which grounds and preserves all finite interactions. They describe where in the scheme of reality this or that action, choice or policy belongs, and thus they direct what we can say about its value and also indicate where we may draw resources for following or resisting certain possibilities. They change what can be said and imagined about humanity. That is why theology is so important – so indispensable, a believer would say – a register for talking about such a range of activities. It recalls us to the idea that what makes humanity human is completely independent of anyone's judgments of failure or success, profit or loss. It is sheer gift – sheer love, in Christian terms. And if the universe itself is founded on this, there will be no sustainable human society for long if this goes unrecognized.

NOTES

1. J. Sacks, *The Home We Build Together: Recreating Society*, Continuum, 2007.
2. Ibid., p. 140.
3. R. Sennett, *The Craftsman*, Yale University Press, 2008, p. 284.
4. R. Sennett, *The Culture of the New Capitalism*, Yale University Press, 2006.

2

INVESTMENT AND PUBLIC POLICY IN A GLOBALIZED ECONOMY

Robert Skidelsky

WHY KEYNES?

At the heart of Keynes's remedy for the deep fluctuations in the capitalist economy was a large and continuing role for state investment. In the *General Theory of Employment, Interest and Money*, he wrote:

> *I expect to see the State ... taking an ever greater responsibility for directly organizing investment [and] I conceive, therefore, that a somewhat comprehensive socialization of investment will prove the only means of securing an approximation to full employment.*[1]

These were the two definite policy proposals of the book. The *General Theory* was not about policy. It aimed to provide an explanation, in terms of fundamental theory, of persisting underuse of potential resources, especially labor. The role Keynes gave the state in investment was a consequence of his "general theory" of employment. It stood or fell by the validity of the theory.

Four immediate observations are in order. First, Keynes's *General Theory* was an attack on what he called the "classical" theory. He took the main assumption of the classical theory to be that market economies had an inherent tendency to full employment. Deviations from full employment were shallow and rapidly self-correcting, in the absence of government interferences. Perfectly competitive markets, *left to themselves*, would always achieve a balance between quantities of labor supplied and demanded. Rather, the main topic of classical economics was the study of the laws governing the allocation of given resources between different uses. As a result, Keynes argued, classical economics had nothing to say about the most serious economic problem of the day – deep economic fluctuations which could result in persisting mass unemployment. His general theory was designed to fill this gap. It sought to demonstrate that the market economy lacked any internal mechanism for maintaining full employment. His purpose was not just to explain the Great Depression, but to show why a decentralized market economy was unable to exploit the full potentialities of production except in "moments of excitement". Keynes would have seen the dot-com boom conditions in the late 1990s as one such moment.

Second, the argument of the *General Theory* was not intended to exhaust the role of the state in the economy. Classical theory had drawn attention to goods, such as "natural" monopolies and public goods, which could be more efficiently or conveniently provided by the state; it also pointed to "imperfections" in actual markets which might justify various forms of state intervention to correct. An important branch of classical economics, welfare economics, was concerned with the equity of resource allocation. Even a perfectly efficient market system might distribute resources "unfairly", justifying government taxing the rich in order to subsidize the poor. Keynes's theory was not concerned with any of these points. This did not mean he thought them trivial: he thought they were of secondary importance as compared to the persistent underuse of resources. He was also concerned to make the political point that state action to secure full employment would be good for both wages *and* profits.

Although Keynes identified "arbitrary and inequitable distribution of wealth and incomes" as one of the two "outstanding faults of the economic society in which we live" (the other being its failure to provide for full employment),[2] his theory was concerned only with the second. He did nevertheless think that a more equal distribution of wealth and incomes would help investment by increasing the "propensity to consume".[3] We will return to this point later.

Third, although state investment was necessarily a national policy (there was no world state), Keynes worked out an "ideal" international monetary system designed to prevent some countries from imposing deflation and unemployment on others. This reflected his – and Britain's – experience of the gold standard from 1925 to 1931. American reserve accumulation had forced the Bank of England to maintain an interest rate which deterred domestic investment, in order to protect its own gold reserve. Keynes thought that "globalization" could only be safely embarked on if countries were not forced to raise interest rates to protect their reserves. The Keynes plan of 1941 for an International Clearing Union aimed to achieve this. As I shall argue, it is extremely relevant today.

Finally, Keynesian theory governed economic policy in the main countries for roughly 25 years, from 1950 to 1975. In addition – and many would say crucially, though fortuitously – US overseas spending, for foreign policy and military purposes, maintained global aggregate demand at a high level. This Keynesian "golden age" was the most successful in economic history, in terms of employment, growth and stability, and much more successful than the "Washington consensus" years which followed. To give just one figure: British unemployment averaged 1.6% between 1950 and 1973, whereas it has averaged 7.4% since 1980. As Thomas Palley argues:

Economic policy was designed to achieve full employment, and the economy was characterized by a system in which wages grew with productivity. This configuration created a virtuous circle of growth. Rising wages meant robust aggregate demand, which contributed to full employment. Full employment in turn provided an incentive to invest, which raised productivity, therefore supporting higher wages.[4]

Nevertheless, the Keynesian consensus collapsed in the 1970s. This was partly due to gaps in Keynes's theory, partly to the way it was interpreted, partly to the way it was applied.[5] What succeeded it as the dominant theory was the "new classical economics", a mathematically updated version of the classical theory Keynes had attacked in the 1930s. It was in the name of this theory and its offshoots that financial markets were deregulated and allowed to grow in the uncontrolled way that brought about the crisis of 2007–09. So Keynes's theory once more confronts classical theory, in a replay of the battle of ideas of the 1930s.

KEYNES'S THEORY

No proposition about the current crisis has been more widely accepted than that it was caused by the mispricing of risk. The mathematical models underlying our recently crashed financial system all assumed that it was possible to measure risk and therefore insure or hedge against loss. Individuals could miscalculate the odds, but, given the assumption of rationality, their mistakes would be randomized. The fact that risks came to be mispriced is attributed to the "mismanagement of risk". Banks failed to manage their own risks; regulators failed to manage "systemic risk" – the risk that the mismanaged risk of individual institutions would all become correlated. The key to the prevention of further crises is therefore better "risk management", by the banks and by the regulators. This whole discourse presupposes that risks can be correctly priced: that somewhere out there, there are "correct" prices from which market prices deviated. These correct prices are said to reflect "fundamentals" or "intrinsic value". On this view, what Alan Greenspan called the "underpricing of risk worldwide" must be due to some failure, or a wilful misuse, of available information. Reforms of the banking system are essentially directed to remedying this set of defects, and, by extension, the "perverse incentives" that gave rise to the latter.

But what if all risks *cannot* be correctly priced? This was Keynes's starting point. He distinguished between "risk" and "uncertainty". Risk is when probabilities can be known (measured); uncertainty exists when they cannot be known (or measured). His original insight was that the classical theory of the self-regulating market rested on a particular epistemological claim: that market participants have reliable information about the future, or, more drastically, that "all things are foreseen from the beginning".[6] Grant this, and the full employment assumption follows; deny it and it collapses. Keynes's economy is one in which our knowledge of the future is "usually very slight and often negligible" and expectations are frequently subject to disappointment.[7] Keynes wrote:

> *The whole object of the accumulation of wealth is to produce results, or potential results, at a comparatively distant, and sometimes at an indefinitely distant, date. Thus the fact that our knowledge of the future is fluctuating, vague and uncertain, renders wealth a peculiarly unsuitable subject for the methods of the classical economic theory.[8]*

Over a large swathe of our forward-looking decisions, we have "no scientific basis on which to form any calculable probability whatever".[9] That is, there is nothing beyond intuition that gives the probability of something happening at a certain time. The existence of irreducible uncertainty is Keynes's explanation for the mediocre secular performance and periodic breakdowns of a decentralized economy. Keynes's theory explains why mathematical models of risk pricing were bound to promise much more than they could deliver.

What was it that rendered large parts of the future impervious to probabilistic calculation? Keynes gave the example of an apple endowed with "human" characteristics. Newtonian physics tells us that it will always fall to the ground, at a speed dictated by the force exerted on it divided by its mass. But no such prediction can be made about the "human" apple:

> *It is as though the fall of the apple to the ground depended on the apple's motives, on whether it is worth while falling to the ground, and whether the ground wanted the apple to fall, and on mistaken calculations on the part of the apple on how far it was from the centre of the earth.[10]*

Some part of the uncertainty attaching to the speed of the apple's fall can be put down to mistakes on the apple's part. However, the main human characteristics with which Keynes equips his apple are "motives" and "intentions". It is these which break the link between economics and physics, and which make economics a "moral" and not a "natural" science. Keynes's point is that economics "deals with introspection and values ... with motives, expectations, psychological uncertainties".[11] The future can't be predicted, because the future is unpredictably changeable. It is unpredictably changeable, in large part, because it is what we choose to make it. As Paul Davidson puts it, the economic world is nonergodic. In other words, the past and the present cannot tell us anything about the future.[12] This view implies a large restriction on the applicability of econometrics. Basically Keynes believed it could be applied only to those fields in which risk is measurable. This excluded most of the risks incurred in investment markets.

The main technique we adopt to cope with a nonergodic universe is to transform uncertainty into calculable risk by giving it numbers. This is what mathematical forecasting models do, using some mechanism to transform an uncertain future into absolute numbers. This gives us the assurance we need to invest. But it is a fake assurance. While repeated betting on horses allows you to update your "priors" to match the "true" merits of the horses, no amount of data on past economic events brings you any closer to their true probabilities in the future because the future is bound to be different from the past. What we do is to use mathematics to *invent* a world of calculable probabilities which we take to be an accurate reflection of the real world.[13]

Thinking about the future as risky rather than uncertain is not foolish. In fact it is the only rational basis of individual action. It is also compatible, as Keynes notes, with a considerable measure of stability. Mathematical forecasts can shape the future they claim to predict, by shaping our expectations. They may produce what economists call "bootstrap" paths or equilibria, paths which are what they are not because the world is what it is, but because beliefs about the world are what they are. They tell a story about the future which gives confidence, as long as nothing happens to shake confidence in the story.

Keynes puts uncertainty to work to explain three inter-linked features of modern economic life: the frequent breakdowns in the investment machine; the role of money as a "store of value"; and the possibility of "underemployment equilibrium".

Why in Keynes's view does investment break down? His answer is that the technique for transforming uncertainty into calculable risk is based on nothing more than a convention, the convention being that:

> *the existing state of affairs will continue indefinitely, except in so far as we have specific reasons to expect a change ... we are assuming, in effect, that the existing market valuation, however arrived at, is uniquely correct in relation to our exist-ing knowledge, and that it will only change in proportion to changes in our knowledge.*[14]

This convention is philosophically flawed, "since our exist-ing knowledge does not provide a sufficient basis for calcu-lated mathematical expectation". Nevertheless, it is compatible with "a considerable measure of continuity and stability ... so long as we can rely on the maintenance of the convention". For, by using the convention, the investor can "legitimately encourage himself with the idea that the only risk he runs is that of a genuine change in the news over the near future", which is unlikely to be very large. "Thus investment becomes reasonably 'safe' for the individual investor over short periods, and hence over a succession of short periods ... if he can fairly rely on there being no breakdown in the convention". Keynes believed that "it has been ... on the basis of some such procedure as this that our leading investment markets have been developed".[15]

But expectations so precariously based are liable to be swept away, because, as Keynes says, "there is no firm basis of conviction to hold them steady", that is, to be able to distinguish between new relevant information and "noise". Suddenly every one starts revising his bets:

The practice of calmness and immobility, of certainty and security, suddenly breaks down. New fears and hopes will, without warning, take charge of human conduct. The forces of disillusion may suddenly impose a new conventional basis of valuation. All these pretty, polite techniques, made for a well panelled board room and a nicely regulated market, are liable to collapse.[16]

This is as good a theoretical explanation as exists for the meltdown in the autumn of 2008.

Money plays a key part in Keynes's narrative of investment breakdown. Holding money is an alternative to buying investments. Keynes was the first economist who clearly identified the role of money as a "store of value". Holding money is a way of postponing spending decisions. What he called "liquidity preference" rises when the "convention" supporting investment collapses. The collapse of investment is simultaneously a flight into money.

Keynes was far from believing that the disturbing power of money emerged only in moments of panic. He thought that throughout history the desire to hoard savings had been stronger than the desire to invest them, because at all times vague panic fears lie below the surface, denting our optimism in the future, and creating a permanent bias towards preserving existing value rather than creating new value. Keynes believed that investment came in bursts of optimism which he called "animal spirits". We can trace these investment upsurges in history – from the railway boom of the nineteenth century to the dot-com boom which ended in 2000. But normally people preferred to hoard rather than invest their money, that is to say, there was a permanently high level of liquidity preference which exerted a permanent upward pressure on interest rates. Hence, Keynes's support for the medieval usury laws which he saw as an attempt to prevent people making money by hoarding money.

Keynes's theory of economic history was influenced by Jevons' famous description of India as the "sink of the precious metals". In the *General Theory* he wrote:

> *The history of India at all times has provided an example of a country impoverished by a preference for liquidity amounting to so strong a passion that even an enormous and chronic influx of the precious metals has been insufficient to bring down the rate of interest to a level which was compatible with the growth of real wealth.*[17]

Keynes believed that from ancient times onwards, the Orient's propensity to hoard influxes of the precious metals had set the Occident a permanent deflationary problem. Shortage of gold in the West had been relieved from time to time by discoveries of gold and silver in the New World, and by Western seizure of Oriental temple and palace hoards. He would thus have seen the global imbalances of today as the reappearance of an ancient pattern.

Uncertainty also lies at the heart of Keynes's theory of persisting unemployment, although this was less developed. As Axel Leijonhufvud has pointed out, the main innovation of the *General Theory* was to create a model in which the system reacts to a disturbance by quantity not wage level or price level adjustments. Following a shock, output and prices both adjust. But prices adjust slower than output because people have no knowledge of the new "correct" prices, even if they exist. When the convention breaks down, there is no auctioneer available to declare a "vector of market clearing prices" before trade starts. Further, only in the very long term need long-run interest rates conform to underlying physical transformation possibilities and inter-temporal household preferences. In the short run, speculation in security markets will make them diverge from levels that obtain under full information. Hoarding and dishoarding are a concomitant of this speculative activity.[18]

This was a frontal attack on the theory of the self-regulating market. Today's monetary theory – as in Keynes's day – suggests that a fall in investment demand relative to saving would bring about an automatic fall in the rate of interest to rebalance the two. But Keynes, as we have seen, thought a great deal of saving was done not to invest but to hoard money, and that this liquidity preference rose during a financial crisis. So the rate of interest in his scheme was the reward of "not hoarding", or, as he put it, "the price which equilibrates the desire to hold wealth in the form of cash with the available quantity of cash".[19] This price might easily stay too high to bring about a recovery of investment:

When a more pessimistic view is taken about future [yields] of investment there is no reason why there should be a diminished propensity to hoard. Indeed, the conditions which aggravate the one factor tend, as a rule to aggravate the other. For the same circumstances which lead to pessimistic views about future yields are apt to increase the propensity to hoard.[20]

Uncertainty may thus cause the real wage and long-term rate of interest to remain for years above the rates needed for full employment. Uncertainty not only brings about periodic collapses, it removes the economy's postulated "self-adjustment" mechanisms. The listing ship does not automatically right itself.

Keynes claimed his theory was more "general" than classical economics because it encompassed a variety of economic situations exhibiting different states of knowledge. The question is: how central is the Keynes case? If the capitalist growth engine is subject to genuine ontological indeterminacy, then its mediocre performance and frequent breakdowns are explained. If, on the other hand, uncertainty can be plausibly modeled as an information problem, to be overcome by learning and by more efficient data processing, then Keynes's case is marginalized, and the classical theory is reinstated as the central case. The comeback of classical economics consisted of marginalizing the Keynes case, and reinserting its own theory of the self-regulating market based on "perfect information" as the "general case".

THE CASE FOR THE STIMULUS

The absence of automatic market self-correction determines a role for government. Consider first the case for the "stimulus". Keynes argued that in a situation of rapid economic decline, it is the government's duty to provide a stimulus – an external source of spending to replace the shortfall in private spending. This usually means running a budget deficit. The extra spending created by government will reverse the initial fall in aggregate demand. As aggregate spending increases, the budget deficit will automatically shrink, since government revenues rise faster than the national income. If the economy starts growing again at its old rate, then provided the budget returns to balance, the increased national debt resulting from the enlarged deficits will also come down automatically. Although Keynes favoured "quantitative easing" (printing money) to bring down short-term interest rates in a recession, he doubted whether the long-term rate of interest – the cost of borrowing to finance investment – could be made to fall sufficiently to offset the decline in investment demand, even if the central bank flooded the banking system with liquidity.

Keynes insisted that it is the spending, and not the printing, of money which has a stimulating effect. Increasing the quantity of money without an attempt to raise demand for actual goods is like pushing on a string. Increasing the supply of cash to the banking system is a way of keeping the cost of private (and public) borrowing lower than it would have been, but it does not ensure a recovery of investment sufficient to restore full employment. Lenders might still demand from borrowers rates of interest for new enterprise which borrowers cannot be expected to earn. So, as Keynes put it in 1932: "there may be no escape from prolonged and perhaps interminable depression except by direct state intervention to promote and subsidise new investment".[21]

It was essential to Keynes's purpose to establish the possibility of persisting underemployment to justify a role for government to improve the equilibrium. A theory of business cycles, even of deep cycles, would not have done the job, since it was always open to business cycle theorists to argue that cycles were part of the normal mechanism of economic progress, and that therefore government action to dampen or prevent cycles was a sin against progress itself. Schumpeter's theory of "creative destruction" did amount to exactly this. An economy stuck for decades in an underemployment equilibrium was much more plausibly an object of special government attention than one whose dynamic exuberance occasionally brought about a collapse.

KEYNES'S POLITICAL ECONOMY

Keynes's permanent system to prevent the periodic breakdown and mediocre secular performance of market economies has three main components: measures to stimulate investment; measures to stimulate consumption; and a reform of the international monetary system to prevent the transmission of unemployment from one country to another.

The first duty of the state is to ensure enough investment in the economy to maintain continuous full employment. Although cutting taxes might give a temporary boost to investment, it will have only a weak and uncertain effect on profit expectations.[22] The surest way to secure enough investment to maintain full employment is to have a large and continuous public investment program. This is what Keynes meant when he talked about a "somewhat comprehensive socialisation of investment". By this he did not mean nationalization. Socialization of investment need not exclude "all manner of compromise and devices by which public authority will cooperate with private initiative".[23] This single throwaway line in the *General Theory* reflects Keynes's thinking on "public-private partnerships" which came out of his involvement in Liberal politics in the 1920s.[24] A steady stream of public investment would reduce the domain of uncertainty to modest dimensions. Such investment would not necessarily be profit-maximizing. But provided it yielded positive returns, there would be a gain. If markets had perfect information, public investment would be inefficient. But, with uncertainty, there is a gain as against having no state investment at all, because of the losses due to uncertainty.

Keynes's political economy would also have used the taxation system to stimulate private consumption, since an "increase in the habitual tendency to consume will in general [that is, except in conditions of full employment] serve to increase the inducement to invest".[25] The rationale for this is that the poor spend a higher proportion of their incomes than do the rich. Marriner Eccles, chairman of the US Federal Reserve Board from 1934 to 1948, spelt out the logic of this position better than Keynes managed himself:

A mass production economy has to be accompanied by mass consumption. Mass consumption in turn implies a distribution of wealth to provide men with buying power. Instead of achieving that kind of distribution, a giant suction pump had by 1929 drawn into a few hands an increasing proportion of currently produced wealth. This served them as a capital accumulation. But by taking purchasing power out of the hands of mass consumers, the savers denied to themselves the kind of effective demand for their products that would justify a reinvestment of their capital accumulations in new plants. In consequence, as in a poker game when the chips were concentrated in fewer and fewer hands, the other fellows could stay in the game only by borrowing. When their credit ran out, the game stopped.[26]

The same "suction pump" was in operation in Britain and the US in the run-up to the 2007 crisis, access to credit compensating for the growing inequality of wealth and incomes.

Finally, Keynes would have wanted a major reform of the international monetary system. The chief need is to reduce the amount of global reserves. Between 2003 and 2009, measurable global reserves have increased from $2.6 trillion to $6.8 trillion – an average annual rate of increase of about 15% at a time when global GDP grew at an annual rate of 4.4%. In 2003, global gold reserves amounted to 7% of total reserves; in 2009, the figure was 12%.

This flight into liquidity amounts to a large increase in deflationary pressure. Reserves are a way of insuring against uncertainty. What is required is to lower the cost of insurance by reducing uncertainty. The best way of doing this is to stem "hot money" flows. This could be done by a "Tobin tax" on short-term financial transactions.

In this context, it is worth returning to the Keynes plan of 1941. The problem which first engaged Keynes before the First World War was how to avoid a hoarding of precious metals by India which restricted its economic development. This broadened into an appreciation, in the interwar years, of how hoarding of surpluses (this time by the US) imposed a deflationary pressure on the rest of the world. His International Clearing Union plan was designed to overcome this by making it impossible to accumulate credit balances in a World Central Bank indefinitely. Creditor accounts permanently in balance would be confiscated, and redistributed to the debtor banks' accounts: a functional equivalent of the more violent confiscations of hoards engineered by such past conquerors as Alexander the Great, Hernan Cortes and Warren Hastings.[27]

No economic policy which took uncertainty seriously would put its faith in floating exchange rates to secure automatic balance of payments adjustment. This is par excellence a market solution which supposes that exchange rates, like securities, will always be at their correct value. This is not the case, with swings in currency values much larger than justified by changes in competitive conditions. So it is important to reach agreement on rules for exchange rates to avoid the adverse consequences of the present system. These deficiencies are two: first, it is impossible for the US to devalue the dollar against the renminbi as long as China insists on keeping a fixed exchange rate against the dollar. Second, the decline of the dollar together with China's fixed exchange rate policy shifts the burden of adjustment onto the eurozone whose currency becomes increasingly overvalued. Keynes would have regarded a solution to the problem of "global imbalances" as key to the further progress of globalization.

CONCLUSION

Keynes was one of the most fertile minds of the last century and much of his thinking necessarily escapes this brief summary. The main reason he placed so much emphasis on the full exploitation of potential resources was that he wanted societies to escape as quickly as possible from the tunnel of economic necessity to the sunlight of the "good life". As he wrote in his essay

"Economic possibilities for our grandchildren", the solution of the economic problem would confront mankind with "his permanent problem – how to use his freedom from pressing economic cares, how to occupy the leisure, which science and compound interest will have won for him, to live wisely and agreeably and well".[28]

NOTES

1. *The Collected Writings of John Maynard Keynes* (hereafter referred to as JMK), Macmillan/CUP for the Royal Economic Society, 1971–89, 7, pp. 164, 378.

2. Ibid., p. 372.

3. Ibid., p. 373.

4. T. Palley, *America's Exhausted Paradigm: Macroeconomic Causes of the Financial Crisis and Great Recession*, New America Foundation, 2009, pp. 3–4.

5. For an account of the causes of the collapse of the 'Keynesian consensus', see R. Skidelsky, *Keynes: The Return of the Master*, Public Affairs, 2009, pp. 102–18.

6. JMK, 7, p. 293.

7. Ibid., pp. 149, 293–4.

8. JMK, 14, p. 113.

9. Ibid., p. 114.

10. Ibid., p. 300.

11. Ibid., p. 300.

12. P. Davidson, *John Maynard Keynes*, Palgrave Macmillan, 2009. The "ergodic axiom … presumes that all future events have already been determined, and cannot subsequently be modified by human action, that is, the future outcomes of any decision made today can be predicted with a high degree of statistical accuracy" (p. 33).

13. Keynes did not believe that expectations turned out "correct" except by accident. What he called the marginal efficiency of capital (MEC), that is, the margin of return over cost, or profitability, is

expected value. Cost is incurred today, the benefit accrues in the future. But there is no connection between MEC and the classical notion of "intrinsic value". In the classical theory, intrinsic value reflected the productivity of the investment: the value added by a new machine over N years. But MEC is not the same as productivity. The prospective yield is subject to all kinds of unknowns. MEC would equal productivity only if the future were known.

14. JMK, 7, p. 152.

15. Ibid., p. 152.

16. JMK, 14, pp. 114–15.

17. JMK, 7, p. 337.

18. A. Leijonhufvud, *Keynes and the Classics*, Institute of Economic Affairs, 1969.

19. JMK, 7, pp. 174, 167.

20. JMK, 14, p. 118.

21. J.M. Keynes, "The world's economic crisis and the way of escape", 1932, repr in JMK, 21, p. 60.

22. The positive effect may come about by increasing the confidence of the business community. Keynes would have been very skeptical of Laffer curve-type arguments that cutting taxes will raise national income by causing businessmen to work harder.

23. JMK, 7, p. 378.

24. See R. Skidelsky, *The Economist as Saviour*, Macmillan, 1992, Chs 7 and 8.

25. JMK, 7, p. 373.

26. Quoted in S. Whimster (ed.) *Reforming the City*, Forum Press, 2009, p. 98.

27. For the first draft of Keynes's Clearing Union plan, dated 8 September 1941, see JMK, 25, pp. 21–33.

28. J.M. Keynes, *Essays in Persuasion*, W.W. Norton, 1963, p. 367.

3

THE COMMON TABLE[1]

Jon Cruddas and Jonathan Rutherford

The financial crisis has taken Britain to the brink. Look down into the abyss and see reflected the country we have become. There is increasingly entrenched wealth for the few, verging on the dynastic in some cases, alongside some of the highest levels of poverty and inequality in Europe. There is more home ownership, but no investment in housing for the next generation and now a scandalous national housing crisis. We live in a consumer wonderland, but stagnant wages have led to unprecedented levels of personal debt. And amid the glittering baubles is a society in which trust has declined, and our democracy and liberties have been diminished. We are at risk of becoming a society stricken by loneliness and increasing levels of mental illness. Our economy grew on bubbles and speculation. Whole regions of the country are dependent upon public spending because business will not invest in the future economy. The boom was a false prosperity that lined the pockets of the business elite. The bank bailout socialized the huge losses but left control and the profit in private hands: did the government nationalize the banks or did the banks privatize the government?

Britain is at a turning point and it is a historical moment that should belong to the left. But financial capital and its ideology of neoliberalism has not been defeated; it has been the architect of its own downfall. The left is floundering in the ideological vacuum left in the wake of New Labour. It has neither the alliances across civil society, nor the collective political agency to secure a new radical electoral agenda. It lacks a story that defines what it stands for. The ideology of liberal market capitalism might have lost its credibility, but it remains the only story of economic life on offer. In the coming decade the left must begin again. We must return to first principles.

A NEW POPULAR COMPACT

The failure of Britain's old model of mass industrial production in the 1960s provided an opportunity for the free-market right to establish a new hegemony. The 1979 Conservative government of Margaret Thatcher broke the power of organized labor, deregulated and restructured the economy, and opened it up to global market forces. Chancellor Geoffrey Howe's 1981 "austerity budget" of public spending cuts and tax increases destroyed the postwar consensus of welfare capitalism. But it was the 1980 Housing Act and the "right to buy" one's council house that helped to win popular support for the Conservative government and secured the 30-year hegemony of neoliberalism.

In the name of a property-owning democracy, a popular compact between the individual and the market took shape. Home ownership aligned the modest economic interests of individuals with the profit-seeking of financial capital. The compact began to displace the old social welfare contract. Change was driven by a state that was itself being privatized, outsourced and marketized. The public sector and civic institutions began to reconfigure their organizations into proxy and quasi-markets governed by cost efficiency and targets. Individual social relationships incorporated a larger element of the rational calculation of the market. Commodification and market relations were extended into society, as this compact of consumer choice and self-reliance was promoted as the antidote to the tired paternalism and condescension of the welfare consensus. It provided a foundational structure for new forms of capital accumulation and the development of a liberal market society of consumers that has transformed Britain.

Economic growth depended on this compact. The housing market became the epicenter of a casino economy that turned homes into assets for leveraging ever-increasing levels of borrowing. The lives of millions were integrated into the global financial markets as their savings, pensions and personal and mortgage-backed debt were expropriated by financial capital. In three decades, GDP doubled, but it was a false prosperity disguising deep structural problems in the economy. Britain's boom was dependent on the imbalance between the huge trade surpluses of emergent economies and the deficits of the rich countries. Despite the extraordinary growth of the financial sector, its business model did not spread wealth and nor did it create a significant number of jobs.[2] The compact established a banking oligarchy which captured both the financial regulatory system and the political class. The business model of shareholder value aligned the interests of a business elite with the market value of their companies. While business productivity failed to grow, the pay of company directors and the senior workforce of the financial houses soared. The credit they sold to middle earners fueled the highly lucrative market in debt securitization that generated their bonuses. In 2007, these totaled £14bn. Gordon Brown, in his Mansion House speech, hailed "the beginning of a new golden age for the City of London". The following year, house prices in Britain lost 13.3% of their value, HBOS and the Royal Bank of Scotland faced imminent bankruptcy and money markets froze.

Britain entered recession in the spring of 2008 with levels of personal debt at £1.4 trillion, of which £223bn was unsecured.[3] The unprecedented levels of debt have created an indentured form of consumption as the capital markets laid claim to great tranches of individual future earnings. The unchecked power of financial capital has also resulted in some of the highest levels of poverty and inequality in Europe. In 1976, the bottom 50% of the population owned 8% of the nation's wealth, by 2001 it had fallen to 5%.[4] In contrast, 1% of the population earn an average annual income of £220,000 and own approximately 25% of marketable wealth.[5] By 2008, 13.5 million people, 22% of the population, were living in households on or below the poverty line of 60% of the median household income of £489.[6] Of these, 5 million are surviving on 40% of median income, around £10,000 a year, a little over two weeks' income for the top 1%. The numbers in deep poverty are at the highest level since records began in 1979.[7] The "right to buy" has enriched many people's lives, but the failure to invest in housing for the next generation has left millions without a decent home.

In a society of consumers, inequality creates a new kind of cultural domination around lifestyle and the conspicuous consumption of status-enhancing goods. Consumer culture became a mass symbolic practice of individual social recognition distributing humiliation to those lower down the hierarchy. The shame of failing in education, of being a loser in the race to success, of being invisible to those above cuts a deep wound in the psyche. Invidious comparisons between one's self and others and between one group and another create feelings of inferiority and chronic anxiety. Richard Wilkinson has shown how this kind of anxiety dramatically increases vulnerability to disease and premature death. Drawing on the findings of neuroscience, he argues that "the variety of physiological processes affected by chronic anxiety mean that its health effects are in many respects analogous to more rapid ageing".[8] As he points out, violence is more common where there is more inequality because people are deprived of the markers of status and so are more vulnerable to the anxieties of being judged by others.

Inequality not only undermines individual wellbeing and damages the life chances of people living in poverty, it increases levels of mental illness across society, undermining trust and creating intolerance. Fear of crime increases. Despite the injustices of inequality, those who gained the least from the economic boom – the poor, welfare recipients, single mothers, immigrants and young people – have all been made scapegoats for anxieties about social disorder and incivility. Economic deprivation has precipitated intergenerational self-destructive behavior, addictions, depression and mental illness, criminality and "conduct disorder", but these are symptoms of incivility, not its root causes. Recipients of welfare benefits have been subjected to a punitive rhetoric that recalls the harshness of the Poor Laws. The New Labour government revived a disciplinary approach to welfare concerned with controlling individuals rather than supporting them. Poverty became an issue about personal behavior and dependency rather than about economic inequality and justice.[9] The problem was not structure or environment but individual failing and dysfunction.

The compact and its ideology of self-reliance and individual market choice not only undermined the welfare ethos, it eroded civic culture, and contributed to the popular disaffection with representative democracy. People have lost confidence in political parties and have disengaged from the public realm. The institutions which have in the past provided access to political ideas and civic activity, such as trade unions, churches and political parties, no longer command the same levels of membership. The 2009 Ipsos Mori Annual Survey of Public Trust in Professions reveals the depth of this crisis of political representation. Only 13% trust politicians, down from 21% in 2008, and only 16% trust government, down from 24%.

CLASS AND COMMUNITY

A dominant belief in recent decades is that a class-based society has given way to a more individualistic, meritocratic culture. In his work on the Third Way, sociologist Anthony Giddens has argued that "detraditionalization" and "self-reflexive individualization" have replaced the valency of class as a social and political category.[10] German sociologist Ulrich Beck has described a capitalism without class.[11] While there has been greater individualization, its development is uneven, not only across class differences in consumption and work, but also within the psyches and cultural identities of individuals. Traditional class identities have fragmented and there has been a significant shift in social and economic risk from business and the state onto the individual. We live in a time not of capitalism without class, but of capitalism destroying class cultures and class relations and recreating them around new modes of production and consumption. Class remains a constitutive part of the capitalist order, albeit in a state of flux and reconfiguration.

Fifty years ago, socialist writer Raymond Williams published a short essay called "Culture is ordinary".[12] It begins with an elegy to his working-class boyhood in the farming valleys of the Black Mountains and the generations of his family who had lived there. Williams describes a way of life that emphasized neighborhood, mutual obligation and common betterment. He belonged to a class that gave him his personal resilience and social anchorage. It gave him a culture and political representation through the Labour Party and a trade union movement. Williams knew that culture was shaped by the underlying system of production. He recalls how from the mountains he could look south to the "flare of the blast furnace making a second sunset". He wrote at a time when his class was already undergoing momentous change, but he could not have imagined the day when there would be no second sunset and the system of production that had shaped his class and culture was turned into scrap. After that, what would come next?

The working class formed out of industrial capitalism has lost its economic function. In Britain in 1978, 7.1 million were employed in manufacturing, by 2008, this had fallen to 3.0 million.[13] With the introduction of new technologies, the industrial workforce in Britain continues to decline. A new global division of labor now transcends the boundaries of the nation state. Goods are increasingly imported from low-wage economies where primitive forms of capital accumulation are creating a global proletariat. Hundreds of millions of extra workers have led to a doubling of the ratio of capital to labor. In Britain, this has accelerated the process of deindustrialization and undermined the income base of the working class. The share of national wealth going to wages peaked at 65% in 1973, by 2008, it had dropped to 53%.[14] To sustain living standards, low- and middle-earning households increased their dependence on capital markets and borrowed. In 1997, the debt to income ratio was 91.1, by 2007, it had risen to 157.4.[15] Millions have been left existing like a reserve army of labor, economically inactive or working in casual, low-paid and insecure employment. Migrant labor has been used by unscrupulous employers to push down wages and working conditions. Work, once a source of collective class identity, has become fragmented and often precarious, making forms of class solidarity difficult to achieve.

In areas of the country, the old patriarchal order of male breadwinner and head of household has been undermined. Not only has this meant poverty, it has lost many men their dignity and self-worth. Sons inherit the legacy of their fathers' humiliation. This cultural destruction of patriarchy has not created equality for girls and women. New jobs in the services sector favor women but they are poorly paid and insecure. Women's earnings remain substantially lower than men's, reducing their life chances in comparison. The destruction of men's jobs increases women's burden as they juggle their roles of main earner, mother and domestic worker. The strains placed on women have made ordinary family life more difficult to sustain, and have reduced their central role in sustaining community ties. For many young people without decently paid work and housing, it has become impossible to leave home and create an independent family of their own. The traditional rites of passage into adulthood – leaving home, getting a job, establishing a family, and taking on legal obligations and rights – have disappeared. The destruction of traditional employment and class cultures has not automatically given rise to new ways of life. It has left many stranded in a liminal existence.

In three decades, traditional class communities and cultures which had provided a defense against exploitation and protection from social isolation have been broken up. It has become commonplace to feel one lives, so to speak, as a stranger outside the community. A people subjected to cultural destruction lose the means to defend themselves against more dominant cultures that seek to redescribe them in negative or derogatory ways. For example, media representations of chavs, feral children, obese men and women, teenage mothers and drunken brawling have been used to define working-class life. As American philosopher Richard Rorty says: "the best way to cause people long-lasting pain is to humiliate them by making the things that seemed most important to them look futile, obsolete and powerless."[16] Cultural difference has become the prism through which large sections of the white population experience and react to the threat to their sense of belonging. Migrants are viewed as competition for housing and underresourced public services. They become the scapegoats for the social dislocation caused by globalization. This culture of blame has encouraged the growth of the fascist UK British National Party (BNP). By promoting culture wars around race, gender and religion, the BNP constructs boundaries of identity that define a sense of belonging and entitlement. Its sentimental nostalgia feeds a cultural melancholy in which the national past always glows brightly as a better place.

SOCIAL RECESSION

Anxieties about cultural loss and the destruction of social ties extends across the political spectrum. In September 2006, the *Daily Telegraph* published a letter signed by over

100 professionals and academics. They wrote: "We are deeply concerned at the escalating incidence of childhood depression and children's behavioral and developmental conditions." Their letter was prescient of a Unicef report, *An Overview of Child Well-being in Rich Countries*, published the following February.[17] It paints a bleak picture of British childhood. The summary of six dimensions of child well-being places the UK at the bottom of the league.

In 2004, the Nuffield Foundation published a study, "Time trends in adolescent mental health".[18] It looked at three generations of 15-year-olds in 1974, 1986 and 1999 and identified a sharp decline in their mental health. Behavioral problems have more than doubled over the past 25 years. Emotional problems, such as depression, anxiety and hyperactivity, have increased by 70%. What the study could not explain was the cause of this trend. It did note, however, that rising levels of adolescent mental illness coincided with improvements in economic conditions. Further studies suggested that these levels have reached a plateau. Causal explanations have ruled out family size. Nor can it be fully accounted for by the increases in single-parent families and levels of poverty.[19] One study, by Stephan Collishaw et al., ends inconclusively with the statement: "Trends in mental health might also be conceived of as a product of both 'beneficial' and potentially 'harmful' societal changes."[20]

Children and adolescents are an acutely sensitive measure of the wellbeing of a society. As they grow, the fabric of conscious and unconscious communications of their families, and, more widely, of culture and class, race and social relations are precipitated in them. They internalize these social relations which come to form the innermost being of individual personality. Problems we associate with individuals – stress, depression, bullying and violence – are dysfunctions that originate in their families and wider social networks. As John Cacioppo and William Patrick describe it: "The social environment affects neural and hormonal signals that govern our behaviour, and our behaviour, in turn, creates changes in the social environment that affect our neural and hormonal processes."[21] Research in neuroscience has demonstrated how poor parenting impacts on the biochemistry of children's bodies, determining their capacity in adulthood to cope with life's stresses.[22] There is now a wealth of evidence that poor attachment or emotional trauma in childhood effects long-term health and life chances.[23] Similarly, feeling excluded and socially isolated undermines people's resilience, optimism and self-esteem and increases their levels of fear, anxiety and hostility.

The neoliberal compact has provided the dominant structuring principle of social life. Its marketized language of customer, contract, choice and utility has pervaded our culture. Social experiences and occurrences are accounted for in terms of what individuals think, choose and do. Individuals are treated as maximum utility-seekers governed by economic self-interest. It is a highly idealized view of human interaction suited to the governance model of utilitarianism and market calculation, but it leaves individuals with no meaningful relationship to one another. A range of disciplines – sociology, psychoanalysis, epigenetics, complexity theory and neuroscience – shows us how this understanding of human nature undermines wellbeing, destroys social connection and impoverishes human potential.

In the wake of the financial crash, the compact that promised freedom through individual market choice no longer commands popular confidence. The old social welfare contract is in tatters, its welfare safety net gravely diminished in value. But there can be no going back to its undemocratic, class-based paternalism. We need to create a new democratic model of the individual living in society. What now is the ethical relationship of individuals to one another and to society?

ETHICAL SOCIALISM

The answer lies in a politics that values the social goods that give meaning to people's lives: home, family, friendships, good work, locality, and imaginary communities of belonging. In our affirmation of ordinary everyday life, we can create an ethics of the common good. It is a politics that begins with us as individuals relating to one another and producing in society. Marx criticized neoclassical economists like Ricardo and Mill who saw the individual as history's point of departure rather than its historic result. The modern epoch that produces the isolated individual is also the epoch of the most developed social relations. In the Introduction to *Grundrisse*, Marx argues that human beings can only individuate themselves in "the midst of society".[24] In his 1939 essay "The society of individuals", sociologist Norbert Elias provides a sociology of this individuality and dismisses the view that individuals are self-contained, "closed personalities".[25] The pursuit of independence as an individualistic project, subject only to rules of just conduct, is an illusion. Human beings are social and emotional beings who are dependent upon other people throughout their lives. As Elias remarks: "What shapes, binds and gives meaning to an individual's belonging is the ineradicable connection between his desires and behaviours and those of other people, of the living, the dead, and even in a certain sense the unborn" (p. 43).

Hannah Arendt provides some philosophical substance to Elias's sociology. She is interested in the fate of our common world: "To live together in the world means essentially that a world of things is between those who have it in common."[26] She likens the "world of things" to a table around which people sit and which orders their relationships with one another. In the same way, a common life both relates people to one another and separates them: "The public realm, as the common world, gathers us together and yet prevents our falling over each other, so to speak. The loss of this realm means that individuals no longer share a concern with the same world of things" (p. 58). Rather than leading to a diversity of identities and experiences, the consequence is the loss of "things essential to a truly human life" (p. 58). "Men have become entirely private, that is, they have been deprived of seeing and hearing others, of being seen and heard by them. They are all imprisoned in the subjectivity of their own singular experience" (p. 58). The problems created by the neoliberal economic order confront us with the need to remake a common life.

This understanding of the interdependent nature of individuals was anticipated by the New Liberals of the late nineteenth century. Leonard Hobhouse wrote: "Society exists in individuals. When all the generations through which its unity subsists are counted in, its life is their life, and nothing outside their life."[27] Like Marx, for whom the individual was a category of relations, Hobhouse described "man" as "the meeting point of a great number of social relations" (p. 85). In his 1898 essay, "The ethical basis of collectivism", he argues that a progressive movement must have an ethical ideal and it must be abstract in that it is not yet realized and embodied in social institutions. One element of this ideal must be liberty but it must find a synthesis with equality, "since it stands for the truth that there is a common humanity deeper than all our superficial distinctions".[28] For Hobhouse, social progress is the development of a society in which "the best life of each man is and is felt to be bound up with the best life of his fellow-citizens" (p. 145).

Hobhouse's social liberalism finds modern-day counterparts in the ethical socialism of Paul Ricouer and Charles Taylor. For Hobhouse, politics is "rightfully subordinate to ethics", it exists for the sake of human life. For Ricoeur, there must be an "ethical intention" central to a politics of socialism. It is "the desire to live well with and for others in just institutions".[29] By living well he means for each person to follow their "good life" or their "true life", which he describes, in terms similar to those of Charles Taylor, as "the nebulous of ideals and dreams of achievements with regard to which a life is held to be more or less fulfilled or unfulfilled" (p. 179). Charles Taylor argues that the ethical value of self-fulfillment has entered deep into modern Western consciousness, but the conditions for its realization do not yet exist. It is, he says, a new phenomenon: "There is a certain way of being human that is my way. I am called upon to live my life in this way, and not in imitation of anyone else's. But this gives a new importance to being true to myself. If I am not, I miss the point of my life, I miss what being human is for me."[30] The concern for one's own identity and self-esteem is social rather than individualistic. It involves the right of everyone to achieve their own unique way of being human. To dispute this right in others is to fail to live within its own terms.

Ethical socialism does not subordinate the individual to the community, nor does it fabricate community where it does not exist. It is about the structure of relations between individuals, which shapes both our psyche and our place in the order of things. It does not pitch the individual against society, but sees individuals as constituted in society. Society has its own kind of regularity, but it is nothing more than the relationships of individuals. There is no "I" without first a "we" that is historical and forged out of culture and society. We no longer live in communities in which people share the same customs and culture, but the ideal of community remains as powerful as ever, because it is about the mutual nature of human relationships. We are a gregarious species and our brains and emotional life do not develop in isolation. Our interdependency is fundamental to our existence.

Ethical socialism addresses the material conditions which give form to individual being. It is a politics of equality founded in the belief that individuals are of equal worth and it is governed by an ethic of reciprocity: "do not do to others what you would not like to be done to you." It recognizes that the task of living necessitates interdependency with others and that this interdependency leads to the question of equality and justice. Ricoeur describes equality as the ethical core of justice: "The unjust man is the one who takes too much in terms of advantages or not enough in terms of burdens" (p. 201). Justice requires not just a singular equality, but the pursuit of equalities around relations of class, sexuality, race and gender. There is no barrier between the individual and society which prevents the transition of ethics from interpersonal life to the social and political realm. Ethical socialism originates in the sphere of interpersonal relationships and extends upward into the wider social realm and into the political community which governs the distribution of resources. Ricouer argues that equality "is to life in institutions what solicitude is to interpersonal relations" (p. 202). Justice holds persons to be irreplaceable and so adds to the solicitude of living with and for others, "to the extent that the field of application of equality is all of humanity" (p. 202).

A NEW POLITICAL ECONOMY

Ethical socialism alone is not sufficient to realize a new society. It must animate radical change in the organization of the economy and its relations of control and ownership. Britain has to make the transition from casino capitalism to a low-carbon, more equitable and balanced form of economic development. The transition demands an economics whose principles are sustainable wealth creation, durability, recycling, cultural inventiveness, equality, and human flourishing. The fundamental logic of this new economy must be ecological sustainability. Climate change, peak oil, the need for energy and food security are all core green issues at the heart of a new economy.

Labour is central to the progressive future and it will need to begin a process of democratic renewal within its own organization and also involve a broad range of progressive social and political movements in rebuilding a centre left coalition. Without this coalition, there will be no organization of political actors and the political agenda will remain unchallenged. This will mean new kinds of transformative political alliances. At its best, Labour has been at the heart of broader social and cultural movements in a mutual exchange of ideas and practices. Without this coalition, there will be no deep-rooted hinterland of support to sustain a future progressive government. It will be quickly blown off course by events. It will buckle beneath the sustained attack of the right-wing media or it will be sabotaged by a conspiracy in the money markets.

In the decade ahead, new forms of production and consumption will continue to reshape society and social relationships. Technology is facilitating new cultural practices and at the same time opening up opportunities for capital to commodify them. New kinds of property and property relations are being created. Just as early industrial capitalism enclosed the commons of land and labor, so the information and communication technology-driven postindustrial capitalism of today is enclosing the cultural and intellectual commons (both real and virtual), the commons of the human mind and body, and the commons of biological life. Government must take on a new strategic authority to check and contain the destructive impact of capitalism. At the same time, it must act as a dynamic builder of the green industrial economy of the future, facilitating a new technoeconomic paradigm across markets and sectors.

We need to develop a democratized, redistributive, social activist, intra-nation state capable of regulating markets and asserting the public interest in the wider economy. It will need to be decentralized and responsive to individual citizens and small businesses. The advocacy roles of civil society organizations, particularly the trade unions, need to be strengthened. We must make capitalism accountable to workers and citizens through regulation, economic democracy and forms of common ownership. Markets need to be re-embedded in society and an ethic of reciprocity re-established in their contractual affairs. The economy must work for the common good. Britain needs an epochal shift from financial capital to production capital to balance its economy and to spread wealth more evenly across the population. Banks as public utilities will need to play a major role in building new homes and in the coming green industrial revolution by directing investment into new markets and into technological innovation and employment. In place of unfettered shareholder value, we must establish industrial organization that fosters long-term investment and real improvements in productivity. We need less financial engineering and more mechanical engineering. The privileging of finance capital has led to the country becoming dangerously exposed to the speculative activities of the City. In the event of another financial crisis, the sheer scale of bank assets and liabilities will put the British state and economy in jeopardy. We literally can't afford the City to operate as a law unto itself. The first task of building a new economy is the wholesale reform of the banking sector and its dominant business model of shareholder value.

In the future, the effervescent quality of wealth creation will demand secure social foundations. The welfare system will have to respond to a flexible and fragmented employment market. We need a nonpunitive, publicly funded welfare system run in partnership with local, nonprofit-making agencies that puts claimants at its centre. The principle of universal benefits has been eroded and we need to begin the long process of recovering it. We can begin with a "citizen's pension" of around £165 a week that would end pension credit means-testing for those over 75. It would be funded using the income-related part of the second pension S2P, instead of pension tax relief. In the longer term, we could think about how the citizen's pension might connect up to child benefit and the child trust fund and so be developed into a citizen's income payable to each individual as a right of citizenship. This would be an unconditional, nonwithdrawable income that guarantees access to the necessities of life. The Citizen's Income Trust calculates that a revenue and cost-neutral scheme can be paid for by a flat rate on earned income of

33% (22% income tax plus 11% employee's national insurance contribution) with a higher rate as at present on higher earnings.[31]

Alongside the productive economy, we need to develop the care economy: a public service of childcare and support for parents, centered on the emotional development of children. Older people need a care system that affords them the same substantive freedoms as others in society. The growing demand for care of older people will need to be paid for and suggestions have included a one-off levy on estates of the deceased. There are new emerging markets and needs around the third age, well-being and health, social care and education. On current trends, this social economy will become the biggest sector by value and employment. We will need to develop novel ways of linking the formal and informal economy. The state needs to be capable of interacting with the complexity and values of social and community organizations, and devolving real power and decision-making to workers and users.[32] Democratizing public services can avoid the problems of the market and bureaucracy and create new spaces of innovation and social development. Achieving a balance between freedom and security, efficiency and conviviality for both workers and users will be difficult, but essential.

A new political economy needs a revival of democracy in order to bring vested interests and elites to account. The introduction of proportional representation in local and national elections has to be a priority in order to reflect the plural nature of Britain. A new system of party funding will remove the influence of rich individuals and interests. We need an elected House of Lords and the revival of local government tax-raising powers in order to deepen and extend democracy through society. These changes will be met by fierce resistance, not only from the vested interests of finance capital and big business, but also from those sections of society who fear they might lose out in a more egalitarian society. Our strength will lie in making deep and enduring alliances and building broad popular movements for change. Despite the disillusionment with political parties, there is an extraordinary level of political, cultural and community activism in our society. Politics has become more individualized, ethical and rooted in a diversity of beliefs, lifestyles and localities. Young people are joining and leading the emerging climate movement. Like early socialism, the new ecological movements are making politics personal and moral. They are asking the important questions about the ways we live and what it means to be human. This is stimulating a search for new kinds of democratic political structures and cultures that will reconnect institutions of political power with social movements and political constituencies.

THE FUTURE

The progressive future belongs to a politics which can achieve a balance between individual self-fulfillment and social solidarity, personal ambition and the common good. It will be one that goes beyond a narrow conception of "the political" to include aesthetic and cultural life. The importance of media, intellectual knowledge, art, music, poetry, image-making and the spectacle is that they give form to new sensibilities and forms of consciousness. They can give voice to the silenced and they create meaning where none has existed before. The activities of playing, dreaming, thinking and feeling make us feel that life is worth living. By returning to our traditions of ethical socialism, we can rediscover a politics rich in emotion and symbolism that will restore ethical meaning and the idea of the common good.

We are now in the end game of an old paradigm. Nothing is guaranteed, but the opportunities for a more ethical politics and economy are real. In the decade ahead, we will need a progressive government that is much more resilient than New Labour in identifying its enemies and standing up to them. Real change will require a strong government that has widespread active support. This can only happen if we build alliances and develop a broad progressive consensus of centre left opinion. Its goals would be a strong, responsive and plural democracy, a restoration of trust and reciprocity in public life, and an ethical and ecologically sustainable economy for social justice and equality. It will be the great challenge of our time, and it will shape the lives of generations to come.

NOTES

1. From the poem 'Te Deum', by Charles Reznikoff, *The Complete Poems of Charles Reznikoff*, Black Sparrow Press, 1976.

2. See http://www.cpag.org.uk/povertyfacts/index.htm.

3. See http://www.creditaction.org.uk.

4. See national statistics, http://www.statistics.gov.uk.

5. M. Brewer, L. Sibieta and L. Wren-Lewis, *Racing Away? Income Inequality and the Evolution of High Incomes*, Institute of Fiscal Studies, 2008, www.ifs.org.uk/publications.php?publication_id=4108.

6. See www.poverty.org.uk. For information about the median income, see http://www.statistics.gov.uk/cci/nugget.asp?id=285.

7. Ibid.

8. R. Wilkinson, "Health, hierarchy and social anxiety", in N. Adler, M. Marmot, B. McEwen and J. Stewart (eds) *Annals of the New York*

Academy of Sciences, 1999, pp. 48–63. See also R. Wilkinson, "The impact of inequality: empirical evidence", *Renewal*, 2006, 14(1): 20–6; and R. Wilkinson and K. Pickett, *The Spirit Level: Why More Equal Societies Almost Always Do Better*, Penguin, 2009.

9. For an example of L. Mead's work, download his 1996 paper, "Poverty and political theory", http://www.nyu.edu/gsas/dept/politics/faculty/mead/Research/Pov_and_Pol_Theory.pdf.

10. A. Giddens, *Modernity and Self-identity*, Polity, 1992.

11. J. Rutherford, "Zombie categories: interview with Ulrich Beck", in J. Rutherford (ed.) *The Art of Life*, Lawrence & Wishart, 2000, p. 39.

12. R. Williams, "Culture is ordinary", in R. Gable (ed.) *Resources of Hope: Culture, Democracy, Socialism*, Verso, 1989 [1958].

13. Workforce jobs by industry, Office for National Statistics, www.statistics.gov.uk/downloads/theme_labour/LMS_FR_HS/WebTable05_2.xls.

14. S. Lansley, *Unfair to Middling*, Touchstone pamphlets, p. 7, www.tuc.org.uk/touchstonepamphlets.

15. Ibid., p. 8.

16. R. Rorty, *Contingency, Irony, and Solidarity*, Cambridge University Press, 1989.

17. *An Overview of Child Well-being in Rich Countries*, United Nations Children's Fund, 2007, www.unicef.org/media/files/ChildPovertyReport.pdf.

18. S. Collishaw, B. Maughan, R. Goodman and A. Pickles, "Time trends in adolescent mental health", *Journal of Child Psychology and Psychiatry and Allied Disciplines*, 2004, 45(8): 1350–62. See also the Nuffield Foundation, *2004 Seminars on Children and Families: Evidence and Implications*, www.nuffieldfoundation.org/fileLibrary/pdf/2004_seminars_childern_families_adolescents_and_wellbeing001.pdf.

19. B. Maughan, S. Collishaw, H. Meltzer and R. Goodman, "Recent trends in UK child and adolescent mental health", *Social Psychiatry and Psychiatric Epidimiology*, 2008, 43(4): 305–10.

20. S. Collishaw, R. Goodman, A. Pickles and B. Maughan, "Modelling the contribution of changes in family life to time trends in adolescent conduct problems", *Social Science and Medicine*, 2007, 65(12): 2576–87.

21. J.T. Cacioppo and W. Patrick, *Loneliness, Human Nature and the Need for Social Connections*, Norton, 2008, p. 11.

22. For an excellent introduction, see S. Gerhardt, *Why Love Matters: How Affection Shapes a Baby's Brain*, Brunner-Routledge, 2004.

23. See, for example, M. Caserta, T. O'Connor, P. Wyman et al., "The associations between psychosocial stress and the frequency of illness, and innate and adaptive immune function in children", *Brain, Behaviour, and Immunity*, 2008, http://www.sciencedirect. com. Also "Stressed parents equals sick kids", *New Scientist*, 21 March, 2008. There are also two reports from the Sainsbury Centre for Mental Health: *Childhood Mental Health and Life Chances in Post-war Britain*, 2009, and *The Chance of a Lifetime*, 2009, both available to download from www.scmh.org.uk.

24. K. Marx "Introduction", *Grundrisse*, Penguin, 1993.

25. N. Elias, "The society of individuals", in *The Society of Individuals*, Continuum, 1991.

26. H. Arendt, *The Human Condition*, University of Chicago Press, 1998, p. 52.

27. L. Hobhouse, *Social Evolution and Political Theory*, Columbia University Press, 1922, p. 85.

28. L. Hobhouse, "The ethical basis of collectivism", *International Journal of Ethics*, January, 1898, p. 141.

29. P. Ricoeur, *Oneself as Another*, trans K. Blamey, University of Chicago Press, 1994, p. 180 (see also p. 172).

30. C. Taylor, *The Ethics of Authenticity*, Harvard University Press, 1997, pp. 28–9.

31. See the work of the Citizen's Income Trust at www.citizensincome. org. See also B. Ackerman, A. Alstott and P. Van Parijs, *Redesigning Distribution*, vol. V of the Real Utopias Project Series, Verso, http:// www.ssc.wisc.edu/~wright/Redesigning%20Distribution%20v1.pdf.

32. See, for example, R. Murray, *Danger and Opportunity: Crisis and the New Social Economy*, NESTA, 2009.

4

THERE IS NO WEALTH BUT LIFE

Phillip Blond

What is remarkable about this economic crisis and the unprecedented economic and ideological shifts it has initiated is that so few saw it coming. Previously, anticipations of disaster were felt 10 or even 20 years before they happened. The First World War was already feared in the 1890s, and the Second World War was already predicated after the end of the first. Likewise, the withdrawal from the gold standard, the collapse of Bretton Woods and, indeed, the final collapse in 1979 of the failing and failed postwar British settlement were all seen by the cognoscenti a good decade before the final denouement.

Not this time though. Advocates of neoliberalism termed the past 20 years or so as the great moderation, theorists speculated on the end of ideology and even history – given the global rise in growth and the seeming defeat of inflation, all appeared ever more rosy in the West's economic garden. Ideology had ended as economic advancement was presaged by a new model of capitalism that was finally going to provide prosperity for all. The crisis of 2007–08, if it was preceded by anything, was indicated by a collapse in the social and real capital of the bottom half of society – the social crisis was accepted in both the UK and the US but only as a negative by-product of ongoing economic success and advancement. But this social recession was the canary in the coalmine; it indicated the crisis to come, for it embedded the contradiction of the current system that by leveraging more and more debt from those least placed to afford it, the neoliberal model would in the end fall victim to its own proclivities.

In the end, this whole agenda was predicated upon the prior destruction of society, for it was only by eroding the political, economic and social independence of society that the economy as construed by the radical libertarians was able to exercise such damaging ascendency. So if we are to truly understand what has and is happening, we must begin with society itself and its destruction at the hands of the market and the state.

In the UK we are facing the disappearance of British civil society. By civil society, I connote everything that ordinary citizens do that is not reducible to the imposed activities of the central state or the compulsion and determination of the marketplace. So defined, it appears that we are now a flat society. By this I mean that there are only two powers in our country: the state and the marketplace. All other sources of independent autonomous power have been crushed. We no longer have, in any effective independent way, local government, churches, trade unions, cooperative societies, publicly funded educational institutions, civic organizations or locally organized groups that operate on the basis of more than single issues. Whatever these various institutions represent now, what they embodied in the past were means for ordinary people to exercise power. These associations helped to give form and direction to human beings; they allowed parents to craft their families and citizens to shape their communities. Nowadays, however, all such sources of independent power have been eroded; instead, these civil spaces have either vanished or

78

become subject-domains of the centralized state or the monopolized market.

The state and the market have advanced from both left and right on virtually all the self-governing and independent domains that previously constituted civil society in Britain. By finding civil society unbearably local, uneconomic or uneven, the market state was able to control and determine its character and so abolish genuine participation in society.[1] This uncritical alliance between the state and the market is highly peculiar. In a uniquely Anglo-American fashion, it was decided shortly after Mrs Thatcher's election in 1979 that the interests of the state and the market were synonymous. All her supporters agreed that to further the interests of the latter we had to restrict the activities of the former, but in order to extend the interests of the market, Thatcher had to increase the power of the state – a logic that was only compounded and increased by New Labour. Both market and state thus accrued power in the name of democracy, and effectively and progressively excluded ordinary citizens from economic and democratic participation. The market has become captured by producer interests along with the state, and, even though both political parties have offered an ideology that pretends that the reverse is true, there can be little doubt that the legacy of both, and of the past 30 years, has been economic and political exclusion for the many, and massive and monopolized enrichment for the few.

Now, though, and perhaps for the first time in almost two generations, the financial meltdown of 2007–08 has given us an opportunity to see the game as it really is. We see that the crisis is due in no small part to the ideological and political complicity between Thatcher and Reagan over capital controls (or the need for abandoning them) and a naive market fundamentalism that allowed the banks to game the state and rig the market. Only now can we glimpse an alternative – one that can perhaps give us a truly free market and a properly participatory state in which citizens feel valued.

British civil society, which is the source and wellspring of our culture, has been flattened by the unleashed authoritarianism of the state and the unrestricted freedom granted to the market. But something had to unleash the state and something had to give free rein to the market. In order for these powers to break all limits and moral restraints, our society had to collapse from within. A stronger civic culture would have permitted modernization and technological development without sacrificing its social foundations. A more active and participatory civic culture would never have let the state destroy every alternative source of power.

In spite of all the propaganda about endless economic growth and the awesome creativity of bankers and financiers, the truth is that, in the 30 years prior to the worldwide debt crisis of 2008, the poor lost almost all their savings and liquid capital, while they and the middle class have taken on unprecedented levels of personal debt. As official statistics demonstrate,[2] the share of the nonpropertied wealth enjoyed by the bottom 50% of the population fell from 12% in 1976 to just 1% in 2003, whereas in the same period, the share enjoyed by the top 10% rose from 57% to 71%. Even when property is included, half the population still owns only 7% of the country's wealth. Clearly, a bad asset situation has, for the worse-off, only become more invidious under the putative benefits of monopoly markets and debt-financed capitalism.

The real outcome of the past 30 years of the left/right legacy is a state of disempowerment. Nowadays we have the worst of the left and the right combined in one philosophy: an authoritarian, illiberal, bureaucratic state coupled with an extreme ideology of markets and the unlimited sway of capital. Little wonder then that most Britons feel they cannot influence their locality let alone their region or nation. Passive and compliant, all we can do is shop – and after a while that doesn't make us particularly happy either.

If only the contemporary advocates of free-market economics could recognize that what we are seeing in our economy is rent-seeking capitalism exercising monopoly and the stranglehold of producers' interests over market mechanisms. Capital has centralized in fewer and fewer hands and is now rented out in the form of credit to those who do not own and so must borrow in order to do so. What we have at present, after 30 years of letting the markets rip, would not be recognized even by the great liberal conservative economist Friedrich Hayek as a free economy – it is Milton Friedman's bastard laissez-faire inversion of it, in which power and wealth flow upwards to the centralizers of capital, the new middlemen who extract a form of rent (in the form of multiple modes of credit) from both consumers and producers, and who exercise such market power that they persuade people that monopoly is in their interest and that renting from them is cheaper and better than owning in its own right. The modern incarnations of left and right have thus, under the guise of the liberal market, strengthened the servile state. The state controls the majority through welfare and tax, while the super-rich, those not bound by nation or responsibility (and let us remember some are), exercise their lordly freedom and their wanton power. If we are to have real freedom and true liberty, the new conditions of serfdom must be recognized and challenged. A revival of earlier versions of a conservatism for the poor, together with a restoration of the social and family structures that alone can truly empower the impoverished and disadvantaged, could lead to a transformation of British society for the better. And here we can find both an economic and a cultural solution to our contemporary crisis. A revived civic culture can only come about as a result of a shift in the British dispensation of power and money. And this will only happen when empowered families and communities start to chart a pattern for their lives that differs from that prescribed by the market state. This will require what might be called a "politics of virtue". Such a politics does exist, nascent within a British tradition that has not yet fully surrendered to the forces that have surrounded it.

One common understanding has it that the financial meltdown was caused by an extension of mortgaged residential housing to those economically undeserving of private property and personal assets and all the economic and social security they bring with them. Framed this way, it seems as if the collapse of the world's financial system lies with the attempt to extend property and assets to the poor. The standard narrative is that inappropriate lending was undertaken, albeit by unscrupulous brokers, and that the system itself is to be faulted only for lack of due systemic diligence. The spurious nature of this argument is not eliminated by its perpetual repetition.

The origin of the present crisis lies not in unwise lending to the poor but in a failure to secure the conditions for a widespread distribution of property. People's desire for security was exploited by propagating insecurity. In essence, a huge transatlantic monoculture of capital and investment was created, into which other nations opted to varying degrees. While creating huge opportunities for trade and investment and vastly increasing the amount of capital that could be deployed for profitable return, this system also reduced all national variations of the market and capital to itself. All capital, whether local, regional or national, became global. Through a growing bubble, more and more money was provided to finance more and more purchases, and house prices climbed accordingly, which in turn allowed a further increase of credit, and so on. This rise in asset value seemed inexorable, such that these high valuations themselves became the source of further valuation and further credit. The ability to pay or finance the debt no longer seemed necessary when so much equity was already in place. Thus, in the name of acquiring an ever-increasing asset value, more and more people became heavily indebted in the hope of acquiring freedom from debt.

The self-augmenting process of speculation was the other mechanism that allowed the bubble to develop. Once trade trades on itself, it becomes entirely abstracted from the real economy. Exchange or nominal value supplants real value in the economy, and the underlying ability to finance or purchase that tradable commodity is no longer questioned. Companies cease to scrutinize these inflated values as a matter of due diligence. They are flying blind.

Historically, if a bank overinvested in a town or a business sector and the economics of that locale or sector changed, then the bank could lose all its loans. Securitization was presented as a pooling of that local risk and a diminution of exposure. In the name of controlling risk, the link between creditor and debtor was broken. In the end, banks and financial institutions were acutely vulnerable to any collapse in the underlying asset base on which so much of their security now rested.

My critique of all the above, drawing on the tradition of Catholic and Anglican social teaching and the work of the

English distributists (as well as on some elements of the ordoliberal and Austrian school traditions), challenges the notion that the aim of contemporary capitalism is to deliver prosperity and property to all. On the contrary, it suggests that what we are spreading is a kind of indentured ownership via ever more extreme levels of credit and that it corresponds, in part, to the analysis of servitude first offered by Chesterton and Belloc early in the twentieth century. For to own something on credit is not to own it at all, and since no security of tenure is available by rent, those who seek some sort of primary foundation or asset in the world have little choice but to buy into a form of ownership that ultimately converts its possessor into a debtor. And there is no "outside" of the market, for to remain external to this economy is to be denied any access to security or prosperity.

The golden age for waged workers in the Organisation for Economic Co-operation and Development was not in this recent allegedly great age of prosperity, but between 1945 and 1973, when they gained the greatest percentage share of GDP for their labor and enjoyed greater real purchasing power. I outline all this in order to show how credit itself derives from an earlier form of dispossession – labor deprived of capital, ownership and security. The desperate drive to attain a stake in the world has for many culminated in a greater loss than they could ever have conceived possible. With over 2 million US homes facing foreclosure and over 300,000 Britons already in mortgage arrears, the misery will only intensify unless conditions ease. In the UK, cuts in interest rates and quantitative easing have driven down the cost of mortgages to levels that people can sustain, but in the US the situation is not nearly so rosy – unable to force down the price of mortgages or introduce appropriate anti-foreclosure legislation, the Obama administration is still courting a catastrophic asset price collapse that may yet plunge us all into another recessionary fall. This outcome, or this dangerous precipice, has been achieved or reached by governments of both left and right, and both state and market have allied to ensure the ultimate monopoly, a universal system of capital that drives wealth upwards and progressively denies the waged classes a purchasing power commensurate with their desire for self-sufficiency and security. That this demand was satisfied and then thwarted by credit is testimony to a capitalist logic of constant insecurity that in its turn generates calls for the servile condition to be re-established and freshly resourced, so as to contain the woes of the newly indigent.

As it stands now, Britain is best characterized as a society that saves income after expenditure in order not to save but to finance debt. For all but the most affluent, Britain has become a *short-term society*, living hand-to-mouth on income, and remaining incapable of using savings to generate assets. Instead, households have used debt to purchase assets, predominately housing, which has created the asset bubble economy that has rendered households so insecure. This trend towards consuming income rather than saving has occurred despite persistent growth in real income over the same period – between 1971 and 2007.

And all this was never economically necessary or structurally required. We could really have gone a different way. Since the earlier economic model was founded on an extreme individualism that requires the state to police the outcome, then the structural links between economically damaging self-interest and state bureaucracy become clear. An anarchic market, which has abandoned trust and eschewed any ethos of the public good, requires a huge state bureaucracy to monitor it and enforce contracts and compliance. The cost of this audit state, in terms of structural overheads and the elimination of productivity, is enormous.

In place of the state increasing the costs of transactions through audit and compliance between two parties that are fundamentally suspicious of each other, we could instead begin to create a civil economy as an inherent aspect of civil society.[3] Such an economy serves society, it both demands and creates trust, and trust so conceived minimizes and reduces the cost of compliance. If the cost of transactions falls, then the regulatory burden on business is reduced, and, if trust becomes the norm, more intergroup ventures are possible and so more business is engendered. The state has too often been the agent of enforcement for an economy of individual suspicion. The radically conservative case for a slimmed-down state is not then what one initially suspects. It is not about the old contest between privatized individuals and a collectivized state. Properly conceived, it represents the first sign of a new mutualism and a different sort of market. With less state, you can have more society, and with more society, you can have a more productive economy. Now that our economy is in such a dire crisis, we should abandon the logic that has led us to both state and market failure. We need instead what both these pseudo-alternatives have suppressed: the economy of a civil society.

For me, the corrosion of virtue through the dominance of liberalism expressed as libertarianism is the deepest malaise of recent British culture, politics and economics. It licenses all the negatives I have outlined above. I now want to consider the possibility of the revival of a modern variant of virtue in Britain.

Virtue is the means by which people fulfill the socially recognized goals they are attempting to reach. Virtue is value and practice combined. If, for example, you believe in love as the basis of human relationships, then you can't treat men or women as dispensable items on the road to your own satisfaction. Virtue also implies a political context for ethics, as it imagines an objectively desirable future, which can only be defined in interrelational terms as a social order that distributes different roles to different people according to their different characters.

How would a new politics of virtue relate to the economy? I argue that we cannot have a moral society without a moral economy, and that a moral economy, rather than inhibiting the free market, is actually its precondition. This argument directly opposes the two dominant ways of thinking about markets and morality. On the neoconservative right, capitalist free markets are seen as ethical exemplars, because nothing is more moral than pure freedom. On the liberal left, by contrast, markets are seen as amoral but necessary – as utilitarian mechanisms for providing certain basic material goods. On this account, truly ethical considerations can only moderate the scope of market influence with nonprofit-making civil associations and state welfare provision.

The problem with the first view is the problem with liberal ethics in general, as already described. Any supposed exaltation of the sacredness of human freedom involved here is exposed in practice as a mask for the justification of the restriction in the freedom of others by the advancement of self. The problem with the second view is that amorality is contagious. If much of life is dominated by naked individualism, this then decisively shapes our behavior. Moreover, modern capitalist markets were only established by seizing control of areas of life that had previously involved only production for the sake of self-sufficiency or else for reciprocal exchange, for example agriculture. These markets sought more profits by appropriating the nonprofit-making sphere.[4] Hence there is nothing stable about the "market sphere" and recent history suggests that its natural desire to extend itself tends to eclipse any well-meaning attempts to limit its functions. These attempts are made yet more difficult by globalization, since local society and national governments cannot hope to contain the global market.

Today it appears more *realistic* to try and achieve a moral market than to limit an amoral market by a more bureaucratic and interventionist state. It is also a far higher ethical aspiration. The liberal left would say that a capitalist market in some things is tolerable but not in others – not, for example, in health, education, human body parts, goods that affect life and death. Yet nearly all commodities affect human wellbeing – whether material or spiritual. Why do we so easily accept a raw competitive trade in food and shelter (without which we could not survive), and yet we baulk at a naked trade in medical care? However, could we not moralize all economic exchanges, without welfare, in various different and appropriate ways? Can we not ensure a basic, just distribution at the level of the economy, thereby minimizing the need for political redistribution in order to correct economic injustices? This is all the more desirable because redistribution is necessarily always limited and unstable, and involves the additional coercion of the state. Besides, because the market logic seeks always to expand its scope, redistribution is a bit like trying to push back the tide with a broom. Welfare merely licenses an original immorality by limiting the market's more unacceptable social consequences and welfarism reinforces a utilitarian, impersonal and individualist understanding of human goods.[5] It is also subject to cyclical cutbacks when the need to regenerate a return on capital once more takes precedence over an equally cyclical need to replenish consumer demand.

For these reasons, then, establishing a moral market is desirable. But what exactly would virtue within the marketplace mean? In the broadest possible terms, it would mean that, while prices and wages would continue to be the outcome of supply and demand, supply and demand would be subject to ethical considerations. This is true to a certain extent today: when we decide what to produce and what we want, we are not only concerned with economic factors. To some degree, people already produce what they think is desirable or have an interest in – people rarely open their own restaurant just to make money, it is also because they delight in the preferential exercise of their culinary and hosting talents. And people discipline their desires not only in relation to their income but also in relation to what they believe to be good for them and for others, as many consumers now limit what they buy to fairtrade or organic products precisely because they do not wish to profit from certain outcomes. I would argue that these other, personal considerations of extra-economic value or sympathy be given social as well as private recognition and become economically valuable as a result.

All the evidence shows that, for most of human history, contract has often had an aspect of mutuality about it, an echo of primitive gift exchange, where the economic bond also established a personal bond, and self-interest did not entirely exclude a concern for the other. Even today this has not vanished entirely: I may decide to shop at my local butcher rather than at the hypermarket because I want to keep that shop's livelihood going, and because I think that small concerns like it are good for the elderly who can't drive and good for the fair treatment of local farmers. Likewise, I may seek out products which are (at least in theory) "fairtraded". It is therefore not a naive fantasy to suppose that elements of sympathy and trust can enter into economic transactions and that the search for an economic good deal can go hand in hand with a search for social solidarity.

The idea of contract as enacting a shared horizon, rather than fulfilling individual, isolated desires can be secured through the idea of the "civil enterprise".[6] In a civil enterprise, there is a cooperative partnership not only between shareholders, managers and workers as stakeholders, but also between these and the regular consumers, who can also enter into partnership in various ways. In this way, the one-sided favoring of the worker – often in a very utilitarian way – by the traditional cooperative is overcome. Instead, the importance of society and of establishing personal relationships can be seen *as goods in themselves*. People come to enjoy their "loyalties" to a certain style of production and product as much as they do the products.

Through civil enterprises, a new type of market regulation becomes possible via shared ethos rather than state imposition. This can come into effect by example and influence – when the ethical firms turn out to be more economically successful than nonethical firms. We need to stop seeing all contracts as amoral and grounded in mutual egoism; once this notion is overthrown, there will be less inclination to form monopolies. This is already true at a local level in many parts of Europe, because small and medium-sized local firms are often content with sufficient profits and a relationship of reciprocity with their suppliers and consumers. The small-scale clothes maker in one northern Italian city is not very concerned about buying out his fellow maker in another town because this would actually compromise his market identity which is closely bound up with the high quality and distinctiveness of his products. It is not that market forces are not operating here, it is rather that qualitative considerations really do enter into market exchanges. By contrast, where the element of sympathy is elided and the typical economic actor is supposed to be indifferent to its employees, its customers and the nature of its products, the logic of the enterprise must be the drive towards total victory and so to monopoly. But at this point of course, market logic has contradicted itself and a competitive market has been abolished. The argument then is that an ethical attitude towards salaries, prices and product quality is actually allied with sustaining market competition, whereas a total refusal of this logic tends to abolish the market in favor of oligarchic corporate control, which tends to become quickly allied to, or synonymous with, the bureaucratic operations of the state.

The neoliberal model of the capitalist market is far too open to the pursuit of bad practice – buy as cheaply as possible, sell as dearly as possible, produce goods with the least possible expense and labor and the shoddiest possible quality. If this gives a market advantage – in part because of uneducated consumers – then gradually bad practice will crowd out good practice and so enthrone bad practice at the expense of the free market itself. But through the proper operation of the market, the opposite effect can be achieved. Good treatment of workers, consumers and products can actually give a competitive advantage, because people will select for social value as well as value for money. In this way, you can achieve a "crowding in of the good and a crowding out of the bad". Good practice and good habits can gradually drive away bad ones. This will not tend to generate a monopoly, even of the good firm, because there is not the same kind of drive to relentless expansion as with the nonsympathetic operator. And before the point where monopolization has been reached, it is likely that good practice will have been copied by other businesses. This then effectively gives rise to a market competition in virtue as well as in profits – and both would be in harmony. The better the product, the higher the social gain and the greater the monetary and societal profit.

Here, then, one can argue something interesting and slightly paradoxical. The logic of monopoly is grounded in individualism, even though it leads to collectivist economic oligarchy. But the logic of anti-monopoly is just the reverse. It sustains some diversity of firm just because, from the outset, it admits more relationality and cooperation.

Thus the civil partnership is a kind of small-scale benign "monopoly" because it involves people banding together who subscribe to certain standards, and by including consumers within partnership, it tends to circumscribe a certain reliable and constant body of consumers who remain mostly loyal. It is only through this relative monopoly that perverse monopolization is prevented, because the ethical business has set up a counter-logic to the crowding-out of good practice by bad. The key to this counter-logic is that good treatment of workers, consumers and products can actually give one a competitive advantage because people will select for quality and reliability as well as value for money.

Once, through all these means, a new economic ethos had been established, it would no longer appear socially or politically acceptable to engage in economic activity in order *only* to achieve a profit without also producing some sort of social benefit.

Given the emergence of such a new ethos, it might well be that at the limit, issues of fair pricing, proper remuneration for work and quality of workmanship could become issues for local rather than central jurisdiction. An economy based on trust can be an economy that requires less state intervention, but it will remain the case that formal contract is something underwritten and only sustained by law. Yet once we have decided that sympathy is both ethically and economically a valid aspect of contract, there is no reason why the law should not also recognize this aspect. Common economic goods should be known primarily through the operations of a "civil economy", but the law would still have a role in securing contracting parties against the worst violations of those goods.

But is all this still not too utopian and in conflict with the proven working of the free market? Not at all. The moral market would alone establish a genuinely free market, since a successful free market, not a market misidentified as a purely individualist endeavor, is in fact already founded upon, and productive of, sympathy, reciprocity and the extension of ownership.

The main reason for this is simple. The free market does not only embrace supply and demand, it also embraces the role of the firm.[7] For a long time, economists have been aware of this, making the fashion for neoliberalism among politicians rather outdated. For neoliberalism recognizes only the individual actor. In consequence, it must view the firm as but an instrumental contractual collaboration between individuals. Viewed this way, nobody within a firm can trust anyone else – and this has increasingly come to be the case within the economic sphere as within the bureaucratic sphere. But if no one can trust anyone else, then much energy must be constantly wasted on everyone within a firm keeping an eye on everyone else and making sure that individuals do not bleed the firm dry as, on this anthropology, they could naturally be expected to do. Of course, this has the consequence of reducing the energy that can be spent on enterprise, while in an atmosphere of distrust, no one's entrepreneurial and creative drive is likely to be fired up and no one's desire to forward the firm's activities is likely to be promoted.

It follows that the promotion of trust is actually in the interests of the free market, just as good moral practice can be ultimately more successful in the marketplace than bad, amoral practice. This suggests, as many economists have long known, that the firm is not best conceived as merely a contract between isolated individuals. Instead, the firm is crucial, as it corrects the inadequacies of the model of classical economics. First, while it is true that the market delivers exact information in a way that cannot be mapped from the centre (as Hayek rightly said), it is also the case that this information often arrives too late to be of use to the individual. I can discover that no one wants my toy wooden horses, but my consequent switch to toy wooden elephants remains a market gamble. This is one reason why individual producers are often at risk from innovation – they simply lack the ability to map the future accurately; instead they tend, if they are successful, to maximize what they do have, which is often a small, reciprocal market. If, however, you have more ambition, then it is better to join a firm (or even start one), not only in order to share the risks, but also because a firm tends relatively to "control the future" by establishing a certain habit of consumption among many people and a better permanent pattern of innovation. The firm is then always in some form already a cooperative enterprise, although misidentified as an individual actor by a neoliberalism that has always misunderstood the economic value of relationships, group activity and sympathy. In this way, the very existence of the firm interferes with the classical individualist "purity" of the market. For, in one sense, the firm reduces competition, since it reduces competitors, but in return produces a higher standard of goods than would have been possible on the basis of a purely individual production. This is why it is firms rather than individuals that tend to be trans-national and successful, because the activity of the group around the common end of excellence and product innovation will always have more ability and capacity than a single individual.

And this is why for the most part I favor mutualist or cooperative structures of ownership and reward. Because the firm is never just the managers – although the managers may be the most important members and so should be rewarded more – it is always a strangely and compellingly communal endeavor. Indeed, where capitalism does not work is where – in the case of mega-mergers for example – managers often game both owners and workers in order to maximize their own short-term advantage against the long-term interests of everybody else. Recognizing this fact allows us to remove the false lenses through which we have been observing economic activity in order to recognize that, insofar as the free market has been *both* successful and good, it is because it already includes the very ideas and notions that I am arguing for. The second reason why the moral market can succeed is that the market is not stable over the long term and does not achieve a perfect equilibrium between demand and supply. Instead, over the long term, any specific mode of supply or demand will tend to atrophy through exhaustion, boredom, change in fashion or failed gambit due to the way in which the market always informs us "too late". A collapse in supply can in consequence lead to unfulfilled demands, while equally a collapse in demand can lead to a crisis of over-production or sterile capital.[8] Against these entropic tendencies, the firm based upon trust again provides a relative surety.

Even classical economics recognized one mode of entropy: the law of diminishing returns based upon "declining marginal utility". This law states that the more we get of something, the less we need it or are excited by it. The fiftieth diamond brooch from the fifth husband will likely bore even the most feverish gold-digger. This is yet another example of the way in which the pure market, as conceived by fully "classical" utilitarian liberal economics, tends to undermine itself in the long run. For sooner or later we all get bored, and for this very reason, John Stuart Mill and John Maynard Keynes in his wake, exponents of this economics, suggested that eventually we will reach a point of satiety when all have enough and a no-growth economy will end the era of economic domination over society. Of course this idea of a final dialectical work performed by capitalism is just as foolish as that of the other great liberal, Karl Marx. For capitalism will engender endless new needs.

But should one then say that a moral economy would be able to discriminate between better and worse need and so would be able to pronounce "enough"? Should a moral economy be anti-growth? Not exactly. Rather, a moral economy can suggest both a way to counteract the law of diminishing returns *and* a more valid mode of unlimited growth.

How is this so? It is quite simple. We get bored by lolli-pops. We get less bored by proper food and still less bored by good paintings and less bored yet by the activity of painting. The same applies to going to the theatre or acting in a play. Creative and relational goods are not subject to

the same entropic processes as ones of mere sensory satisfaction.[9] And yet these are still commodities in one of their
aspects. Hence, the more an economy is turned towards
the production of creative and relational goods, the more
it counteracts diminishing returns. In this way too, a more
moral economy is a more stable market economy. Yet at
the same time, we can see how the infinite growth of such
goods is only to be welcomed, since they enhance rather
than destroy our natural and social environment.

In essence, liberal market economics is based upon individualism but generates monopoly. It theorizes stability
but generates entropy. By contrast, an economy of virtue
guards against both monopoly and entropy in the multiple ways that we have seen. Likewise, a liberal economy
tends to promote centralization, whereas an economy of
virtue protects both the locality and the center. This is
because the "circle of trust" tends to extend only so far, or
if it reaches round the world, in the case of a big corpor-
ation, it does so in a way that is not trying to destroy all
local enterprise and all local integrity. Indeed, the model
for future corporate activity is exactly this: a sympathy
between the things that only a transnational can produce
and the locality and economy in which they are manufac-
tured. Thus corporates will make and market products for
the regions they are in and try to produce a diversity of
suppliers, not least because that builds economic resilience
into the supply chain and extends the benefits of ownership and trade to more actors.

An economy of virtue promotes a "principle of economic subsidiarity", which favors production and delivery
at the geographical level and in the mode (profit or
nonprofit) that is most appropriate for businesses and
society. In both cases, a new kind of market advantage
can accrue because the economic gain from sympathy

extends not just horizontally between players at the same level but also vertically between enterprises of different size and scope. This makes markets that include sympathy more not less productive. Certainly, we must always guard against a local protectionism that could deny access for local consumers to more desirable or more excellent products from elsewhere. But the demand for such protection often stems from illegitimate and state-sanctioned subsidies that impede a competitive and open market. By contrast, a truly competitive market would allow and license competition between localities, rather than the current situation where all too often it is just transnationals which can compete while local enterprises cannot. Indeed, it is the development of the infrastructure of mass trade in the market economy and the collapse in the price of transaction and transport that allows, perhaps for the first time, a genuine global competition between localities.

Hence the final paradox is that the dominance of the individualistic profit motive ultimately destroys the market, whereas commerce as a mutually sympathetic endeavor sustains it in perpetuity. The free market is the upholder of genuine liberty on the basis of reciprocal exchange.

If our economy essentially collapsed by destroying society as the ultimate arbiter of the good, then only a reintegration of economy and society can heal the wound and deliver a cure. The elevation of society above economy and the creation of a moral market is then the only genuine alternative to the continued destruction of wealth, both financial and social. There is no wealth but that enshrined in the good life and the extension of that to all subjects and all citizens.

NOTES

1. As a concept, "liberal capitalism" doesn't really capture the extraordinary nature of this alliance between political and financial power. Nor does the expression "laissez-faire" capture the current phenomenon, since in both terms, there is nothing liberal or free about what is going on. Better I think to try to capture the element of drive and compulsion that is at work in this process. To that end I shall call Britain and America market states, as this seems to encapsulate better the current coercive nature of the relationship between society, the state and the market. See P. Bobbitt, *The Shield of Achilles: War Peace and the Course of History*, Knopf, 2002. I do not, however, endorse all of Bobbitt's analyses.

2. See http://www.statistics.gov.uk.

3. L. Bruni and S. Zamagni, *Civil Economy: Efficiency, Equity, Public Happiness*, Peter Lang, 2007.

4. See M. Perelman, *The Invention of Capitalism*, Duke, 2000.

5. See K. Polanyi, *The Great Transformation*, Beacon, 2002.

6. See Bruni and Zamagni, op. cit.

7. See E. Screponti and S. Zamagni, *An Outline of the History of Economic Thought*, OUP, 2005.

8. See Screponti and Zamagni, op. cit.; H. Arendt, *Imperialism*, Harvest, 1976; R. Brenner, *The Boom and the Bubble*, Norton, 2002. Although Brenner's overall analysis is questionable, he is good on the issue of unrealizable capital.

9. Bruni and Zamagni, op. cit., pp. 239–45.

5

THE KNOWLEDGE ECONOMY, ETHICS AND THE CHALLENGE OF DIVERSITY AFTER THE CRASH

Adam Lent

INTRODUCTION: THE RETURN OF INDIVIDUALISM VERSUS COLLECTIVISM

Having been asleep for over 20 years, the old battle between individualist and collectivist has been woken by a crash. Suddenly, a debate, which seemed to have been settled in favor of the individualist point of view, has sprung back to life.

The Labour Party, where activists were long ill at ease, if largely quiet, about the Blairite accommodation with the individualism of the Thatcherite era, is now enjoying a so far civilized debate between those who enthusiastically urge a liberal republicanism[1] and those who look forward to a more solidaristic society.[2]

Most interestingly, however, the debate has reared its head with equal intensity in the Conservative Party. While the neoliberal love of free markets populated by forthright, enterprising individuals lives on, a new strand of "progressive conservatism" strikes a forceful communitarian note, laying a stronger emphasis on mutualism rather than the market as the alternative to the state.[3]

But the themes and tropes of the debate also pepper, almost unconsciously, swathes of our post-crisis public discourse. The opprobrium piled on the bankers is not just about their undeserved rewards. It is also about the sense that it is wrong for one wealthy group to divorce themselves from their wider national community and buy lifestyles of privilege and power beyond the imagination of the vast majority. At some deep level, we resent the fact that they have shuffled off the responsibilities, if not the benefits, of community life in order to pursue their individual desires.

The rising public deficit, a direct result of the crash and recession, has also created a battle that is tacitly about the responsibilities to the collective in hard times. For the left, the "pain must be shared equally", which usually means the wealthy need to pay higher taxes to address the deficit. For the right, the pain must be borne by a swollen public sector, which, unlike the majority, is still enjoying the good times while everyone else suffers. That was at least one of the meanings behind George Osborne's heavily loaded and highly communal phrase: "we're all in this together."

It is not difficult to understand why in a time of political uncertainty and economic stress we should return to this debate. Its themes have been rerun many times in many philosophical disputes since industrial capitalism and the modern state first emerged. The contrast between individualism and collectivism structured Protestant and Catholic tensions, urban and agrarian disputes, the capitalist and socialist clash of the twentieth century, the Conservative and Labour battles of the prewar and postwar era and, more recently, the libertarian and communitarian debate. And, of course, it colors many, many other deliberations in spheres as diverse as ethics, economics, psychology and culture, to name but a few.

Maybe, as some would have it, the debate recurs because it reflects something fundamental about human nature. Maybe it recurs due to a path dependency in the concepts and language that structure our thoughts about the world. Whichever it is, the debate is clearly profound and compelling.

THE INFLUENCE OF POSTWAR BRITISH HISTORY

There is a further factor which makes this dispute particularly resonant in the UK. That is the narrative that dominates our understanding of British postwar history and the major cultural, political and social transformations that have been closely linked to the major economic shift of this period – from an economy built primarily on manufacturing industry to one built on services. In this narrative, we have (apparently) had around 30 years of a politics, society, culture and economy that veered towards the collective end of the spectrum, followed by around 30 years that veered towards the individualist end.

The period from the mid-1940s to the late 1970s, so the story goes, was characterized by strong neighborhoods, strong civil society institutions, such as trade unions, churches, working men's clubs, the Women's Institute and the Rotary Club. In addition, the politics were unashamedly social democratic, based on high taxes, large-scale social provision and nationalized industries – we had big collective obligations and we got a lot back in return. Culturally, as well, people did things en masse: football crowds were vast, political demonstrations were vast, individual radio and TV programs got vast audiences. It was also a period of a more pronounced courtesy based on mutual respect, particularly in the public realm.

From the early 1980s, it is often claimed, a new ethos took over with some rapidity. Within a few years of Mrs Thatcher winning her first election, the yuppie was born and suddenly personal wealth became a national obsession. "Greed is good" was the watchword and things began to fragment. Neighborhoods lost their community spirit and instead became merely one element in the calculation of your house price. The old associations went into decline, cultural forms fragmented and public spaces became spheres to negotiate fearfully. The social democratic state was rolled back for the good of the consumer, leaving workers, employed or otherwise, to sink or swim. Ultimately, a breed of ultra-yuppie evolved in the banking sector in the first decade of the twenty-first century and brought the whole thing crashing down in September 2008.

Other stories exist. For some, Act One of our postwar history was indeed more collective but it was a horribly stifling communitarianism of enforced morality under-pinned by sexism and a hatred of difference that saw black and Asian immigrants and gay people facing discrimination and persecution. Act Two began not in the 1980s but in the 1960s when difference and individuality began to be accepted and even celebrated. Others, on the right, seem to agree with this broad historical division but worry that the cultural revolution of the 1960s, rather than the 1980s, gave rise to many of the problems that the left ascribe to Thatcherism.

But whatever one's political outlook, or whichever decade one takes as a turning point, the duality in the narrative is clear: an earlier postwar period characterized by collectivism and a later post-1960s (or 1980s) period characterized by individualism. It does not matter whether these narratives are correct or not, they clearly shape our current views about what is possible and what is good or bad. Most importantly, they give the force of historical "reality" to the duality between individualism and collectivism that shapes our current debates. Few, either on the left or right, believe we can (or should) go back to the 1950s, or believe that everything from 1979 onwards was utopia, but this narrative gives all sides a strong sense of what has been lost and what has been gained – it provides an indispensable feel for the approximate things we are fighting for or against. In short, the narrative inspires. So it shapes our debates right now when the prevailing consensus has been replaced by something of a vacuum since the crash.

It is the contention of this essay, however, that this duality is failing us. It fails us at an ethical level and at an economic level. It is not that it has necessarily always failed, but, given the realms of what is now possible and what is now needed, it does.

To be clear, this essay does not argue that we need to strike a balance between individualist and collectivist approaches. That has been a contention of every side in the debate for many years – there are few now who believe that the inescapable communalism of the kibbutz or the unrestrained individualism of the novelist and philosopher Ayn Rand offer serious ways forward. The debate has always been about where one is placed on a spectrum. The argument presented here is that we need now to make the effort to think beyond this tension and instead begin to create a politics based on a radical ethic of diversity, which can embrace both individualist modes and collective modes of life (and the variations in between) and operates simultaneously and/or at different times in a person's life. This, it is argued, is more likely to produce an ethics linked to genuine human flourishing and is more beneficial for the economic life of an economy built on knowledge and services.

INDIVIDUALISM, COLLECTIVISM AND THE FAILURE OF INDIVIDUALITY

Both the more individualist and more collectivist strands may accuse each other of lacking ethical foundation but in truth they both believe they are deeply rooted in complex ethical principles which enable human flourishing in one form or another.

For the individualist, flourishing can only come through exercising our human reason to make choices about our beliefs, our actions and our lives. The greatest threat to the exercise of that reason comes from the tendency of the state and wider society to control the values and behavior of others and to enforce conformity and dependence. Therefore, flourishing can only be built on an institutional, cultural and economic guarantee of the freedoms and rights that protect the individual against the predations of state and society. There is an important ethical flipside to this which is the expectation, or even obligation, that free individuals will exercise responsibility for themselves and their families through hard work and will engage in serious thought about their values and life choices.

For those of a more collectivist mindset, flourishing comes through the identity, practices and protections offered by engagement with a community. Individuals, whether they like it or not, are creatures of their social setting – to cut oneself off from that social setting is to deny one's humanity and to deny the best that humans can achieve through cooperation and mutual support. This requires an ethics of commitment to, and even sacrifice for, the common or public good. At root, it is about respect for and care for others, sometimes at a cost to one's own short-term individual interests. Most importantly, for the collectivist, straying too far towards an individualist approach (and the implications this has for the maintenance of social protection and guarantees against exploitation) will leave large parts of the population without the basic material means to live decent lives and hence will fatally undermine their capacity to flourish even in the way the individualist claims is crucial.

Of course, as pointed out above, these are philosophical touchstones that inform wider world-views, not absolutes. However, it is foolish to pretend that these idealized understandings of human flourishing do not profoundly inform the demands and style of different sides in political debate.

The problem has arisen, as it so often does, in practice. The history of the practical application of these two strands is littered, of course, with both success and failure sometimes operating at the very extremes of human achievement and human degradation. But the UK's own postwar history offers its own insights that are most relevant to the current conjuncture.

Leaving aside the stylized narratives above, there are some important facts about both phases in our postwar history that are verifiable. The three decades after the war did enjoy higher levels of equality[4] guaranteed by the state and well-embedded processes of workplace bargaining. It is also a period that suffered less crime[5] and less family breakdown.[6] And, at least until 1974, it was a period that did not suffer any prolonged economic recession. Finally, engagement with the democratic process was much greater, with higher election turnouts and much larger party memberships.[7]

However, it is also a matter of well-established record that it was a period of extended austerity (certainly into the mid-1950s) and of much greater conventionality, which assigned firm gender and generational roles, rigid class stratification and was generally fearful of difference in the form of sexuality, disability and race.[8] It was also an era that ended in a decade of economic uncertainty in the 1970s, characterized by stagflation, stop-go economics and deteriorating industrial relations.

The social and cultural revolution that began in the late 1950s and became a major national and global phenomenon in the following decade, which was joined by an economic transformation in the 1980s, was a very conscious backlash against the restrictions of this postwar period. The result, over some years, was a greater emphasis on individual freedoms in many spheres, a much greater cultural openness to people from different class backgrounds, and extended rights and freedoms for women, gay people, disabled people and ethnic communities. This was also a period of quite extraordinary innovation and expansion in the services provided by commercial organizations to consumers as well as the rapid growth of information technology (IT) and telecommunications, with all the benefits that has brought in terms of productivity, convenience, information-sharing and human connection across the globe. The result has been periods of sustained and high economic growth, with a consequent rise in living standards and affluence, particularly between the mid-1990s and late 2000s.

The downside has been well documented: inequality and poverty have risen since the early 1980s,[9] the economy has been less stable, suffering three major recessions and a series of serious financial crises over the same time period, and there seems to have been a deterioration in the social fabric, with more people reporting lower levels of trust[10] and figures showing higher crime rates than the earlier postwar phase.[11]

But perhaps the most striking, and often unacknowl-
edged thing about this latter period of heightened individualism, in the context of this essay, is how large
numbers report feeling stifled and constrained by predominant modes of life in a way that bears similarities to the
earlier period. Without doubt, today there is greater toler-
ance, even celebration, of difference and this is the result
of the political struggles around issues of gender, sexuality
and race in the 1970s and 80s, but also the result of a
heightened acceptance of individual choice that grew
directly out of the greater emphasis on individualism that
took hold in the 1960s and 80s. But many feel that a
culture of overwork and accumulation has emerged in
recent years, which leaves people stressed, with limited
time for more meaningful pastimes and their families and
too focused, often against their better judgment, to prove
themselves through individual material success.[12]

It is as though our emphasis on homogeneity and
convention in the more immediate postwar phase stifled
individuality through various legal restraints and peer pressure, but that, ironically, our emphasis on individualism in
the later phase has stifled individuality through increased
pressure at work and a commercially driven culture that
urges self-validation through material accumulation.

But we should also be clear that this is not just about
cultural pressures: the economic imperatives requiring
people to join this mode of life merely to survive have also
proven very strong. The rise in house prices, the decrease
in local shopping facilities, and the fall in wages relative to
the rise in productivity, profits and investment[13] mean that
a culture where both partners work, where home ownership is ever-harder to attain, where two cars per family are
often required, and where, inevitably, personal debt piles

up mean that participation in the culture of overwork and accumulation is not a choice but a necessity.

This paradox at the heart of post-1980s individualism is highlighted further when we consider how far this new set of constraints is from the vision of Britain's most influential sage of individual freedom – John Stuart Mill. It is clear from his seminal work, *On Liberty*,[14] that Mill was not making a plea for the freedom to enjoy individual sensual pleasures through material accumulation. His hope was for a world where people were free to live according to their own reason and, put simply, to do things differently no matter what the state or society (or, for that matter, the economy) wanted them to do.

There is one important chapter in *On Liberty* entitled "On individuality, as one of the elements of well-being". Mill is clear in that chapter that one of the chief reasons why we should secure individual freedom from interference is because this will allow us to become fully rounded humans. He sums this up in the pleasing aphorism: "It really is of importance, not only what men do, but also what manner of men they are that do it".

He writes:

He who lets the world, or his own portion of it, choose his plan of life for him, has no need of any other faculty than the ape-like one of imitation, he who chooses his plan for himself, employs all his faculties. He must use observation to see, reasoning and judgement to foresee, activity to gather materials for decision, discrimination to decide, and when he as decided, firmness and self-control to hold to his deliberate decision. (p. 34)

To emphasize the point, Mill approvingly presents a quote from Wilhelm von Humboldt:

the end of man, or that which is prescribed by the eternal or immutable dictates of reason, and not suggested by vague and transient desires, is the highest and most harmonious development of his powers to a complete and consistent whole. (p. 33)

And for Mill, this more rounded individual can only arise when the option of a deep diversity is present. He calls for a society in which there can be "different experiments of living" and where "different modes of life should be proved practically". In one of the most striking passages on the subject, he states:

In this age the mere example of non-conformity, the mere refusal to bend the knee to custom, is itself a service. Precisely because the tyranny of opinion is such as to make eccentricity a reproach, it is desirable, in order to break through that tyranny, that people should be eccentric. Eccentricity has always abounded when and where strength of character has abounded; and the amount of eccentricity in a society has generally been proportional to the amount of genius, mental vigour, and moral courage which it contained. That so few now dare to be eccentric, marks the chief danger of the time. (p. 39)

Given the trajectory of Britain's past few decades, Mill poses a brilliant and challenging question: can we say that, in either phase of our postwar history, we have really created a society in which eccentricity is allowed and even encouraged? We know this was clearly not the case in the immediate postwar period, and we now know that, despite the advances in toleration and various freedoms since the 1960s and 80s, a new type of constraint has arisen that traps people into a culture of material accumulation and overwork.

If Mill were to emerge from philosophers' Valhalla today, he may feel greatly encouraged to see the differences that do exist between early twenty-first century Britain and the constrained, impoverished Victorian era he knew. But one wonders whether a greater doubt and dispiritedness might not take hold over time as he began to understand the pressures and restrictions that underpin this apparently diverse and vibrant society we live in. He may ultimately be shocked to conclude that von Humboldt's vision of a society of humans whose choices are "prescribed by the eternal or immutable dictates of reason, and not suggested by vague and transient desires" has not emerged after 30 years of the apparent expansion of individual freedom.

THE ECONOMICS OF DIVERSITY

Both the more individualist and more collectivist strands believe that their attitude to economics are built upon profound, universal truths about human interaction and flourishing. On this basis, those of a more individualist inclination regard the decades immediately after 1945 as an aberration, while collectivists see the era ushered in by Margaret Thatcher as deeply flawed. Of course, the strength of feeling towards these periods is determined by one's position on the individualist/collectivist spectrum.

However, the work of Carlota Perez, theorist of economic history, casts these periods in a rather different light.[15] Perez shows that the patterns of economic development which have characterized industrial capitalism since its inception are inescapably bound up with complex but broadly repetitive shifts in attitudes to business, society and culture.

For Perez, the 30 or so years after the war were symptomatic of the decades that have tended to follow the four major financial crashes that have occurred since the mid-eighteenth century. In these periods, the pre-crash dominance of finance capital is ended. As a result, the state tends to play a more significant role as investor and as economic planner. In addition, profits have to be generated through a painstaking search for productivity within firms through the application of contemporary technologies and new business paradigms rather than through financial engineering and finance-led investment. The result often is a period that places greater stress on national solidarity, collective effort and workplace innovation and commitment.

This economic and cultural shift takes very different forms in different eras, often determined by the new business paradigm in play. In the postwar period, it was built around a social democratic vision of a nation healed through greater fairness and the creation of new mass markets, based heavily on the creation of a decently paid working class enjoying the fruits of a new workplace settlement centered on collective bargaining. This worked well with a paradigm of industrial production built around the technologies of mass production which could achieve, through the large-scale Fordist structure, much higher levels of productivity and output but only limited diversity in the commodities they produced.

The more individualist turn that began in the 1980s was closely linked to the re-emergence of a vigorous financial sector that itself was spurred by the IT revolution that began in the early 1970s and the linked changes in production and distribution techniques that raised productivity – a close relationship between finance and the IT transformation of the economy that was to end in 2000 with the dot-com bust.

Perez's analysis shows that the political and cultural collectivism and individualism that characterized the two phases of our postwar history cannot be divorced from a complex relationship with the economic patterns and paradigms that shaped those eras.

If Perez is right, then the 2008 crash (which she acknowledges as the fifth of the big crashes that have shaped industrial capitalism)[16] opens up the possibility of a shift away from the individualism of the post-1960s/1980s conjunctures. However, before we assume this means a return to the collectivism of the earlier postwar era, we must consider the very different business paradigms that now influence our world.

The major distinction between the business paradigm that shaped the earlier period and that of today is the issue of heterogeneity. As mentioned above, the great breakthrough of the technologies and paradigms developed in the 1910s (and which shaped business as late as the 1970s) was the Fordist model, which discovered how to produce a great deal of rather similar products at a much cheaper price than was previously possible. The investment frenzy generated by this technology and paradigm ultimately led to the Wall Street Crash of 1929 but also created the mass markets that developed in the postwar period.

The breakthrough delivered by IT (generally regarded as beginning with the launch of the Intel microchip in 1970) was to introduce much greater heterogeneity into the process of mass production and distribution. This shift led to a culture of consumer choice that was unthinkable in the 1950s, a dizzying fragmentation of markets into an ever-increasing number of niches, the rise of highly customizable products in both manufacturing and services and, now, through the internet, the creation of services in which the commodity is little more than a template within which the content is generated by the consumer themselves.

This paradigm cannot be ignored if we are trying to understand what sort of politics might follow the crash, especially if Perez is right that the paradigm will soon become even more influential and deeply embedded in the economy.

The truth is the type of solidarity that existed in the postwar era will not return in anything like the same form because the underpinnings of large-scale production facilities, mass markets and associated cultures, and the creation of a very large public sector modeled on the homogeneity of the contemporary business paradigm will not return either. It is the tendency to heterogeneity in the economy that will grow, possibly at an even faster rate, now. As the financial sector proves unable to generate the super-profits it once did, the pressure will be on companies in other sectors to adopt the most innovative technologies and approaches to raise productivity and all the momentum here is behind offering consumers more choice and power.

But nor does this simply herald a continuation of atomized individuality and material accumulation. One striking thing about the most cutting-edge aspects of the new technology and paradigm is the way it sponsors both individualist and collectivist expression and, more often than not, modes of interaction which are hard to characterize as either. Twitter and Facebook, for example, have proved themselves conduits for the some of the most crass and self-centered exhibitions of individualism possible. But, at the same time, they have been highly innovative tools in the creation of new communities with shared interests and values and have been absolutely central to the creation of collective action designed to bring about change in the nonvirtual world – the most notable example, so far, being Twitter's continuing role in the current Iranian dissent.

But it is the open source movement that presents maybe the most significant challenge to the simple duality of individualism and collectivism in this economic phase. The open source creation of software on the internet has not been a marginal affair. Programs such as Unix, Linux, Apache and Wordpress have been fundamental to the growth and workings of the internet and thus to the vast economic opportunities and transformations it is creating. The key feature of these products is that they are free to use and so have allowed the internet to grow at a speed and achieve a level of accessibility which would not have been the case were they as costly as other programs produced by the normal corporate route.[17]

The reason they are free is because all the research and development was conducted by software specialists and users employing their expertise and experience to produce a "marketable" product entirely voluntarily through online communities. The same process is continuing with a variety of other products which could prove transformatory and through the many wikis which use online expertise freely given to produce complex sources of information for other users.

Is this sort of activity individualist or collectivist? It is not entirely clear. At one level, people are cooperating in a joint endeavor without any personal pecuniary benefit. But at another, the engagement can be highly atomized, with participants simply feeding back views rather than taking part in an ongoing and complex dialogue (although that can happen as well). Furthermore, this is endeavor that creates tools which can be put to both highly collectivist activities (organizing a local club on the Web) and highly individualist activities such as selling items to generate cash. And there is often a money-making scheme at the heart of an open source project. For example, the basic versions of open source software may be free but charges can apply to more sophisticated versions.

Even the motivation of participants is unclear. Do wiki participants edit pages or post items because they see themselves as taking part in a worthy collective effort or because they derive some personal satisfaction from seeing their work on show? Do they feel a kinship with the rest of their wiki community or are they trying to shape that community's views in line with their own world outlook? It is unclear and the truth probably encompasses all these motivations.

As such, the best way to understand this new technology and new paradigm in a post-crash environment is to see it as expressive of a human tendency to diversity rather than essential individualism or essential collectivism. It seems, at this early stage of its development, to provide a more complex mode within which people are free to choose individual and collective modes of operation as well as modes which do not fit neatly into either.

CONCLUSION: LIVING UP TO THE CHALLENGE OF A NEW DIVERSITY

Could this mean that we might finally break with the two phases of postwar British history, each stifling and constraining in their own way, and come closer instead to Mill's hope for a society in which there can be "different experiments of living" and where "different modes of life should be proved practically"?

Despite Perez seeing technology and associated business paradigms as central to the various developmental phases of capitalism, she is no determinist. Those factors set the broad frame but there is a large space for a wealth of historical contingency to influence how they affect wider politics, lifestyles and cultures. In short, the confluence of the crash, modern technology and innovative business paradigms may offer an exciting opportunity to create a new diversity but it will only happen if those with a genuine interesting in human flourishing seize that opportunity and turn it into something profound.

In this spirit it is worth considering what an ethic and a politics of diversity might look like in more detail at an individual, organizational and state level.

At an individual level, an ethic of diversity is somewhat different to much of the debate we are currently having about individual behavior. In the individualist/collectivist discussion in the wake of the crash, there is much debate about how a person can achieve the "good life" by orienting themselves more towards their community or towards their own individual and family interests.

An individual ethic of diversity would logically reject any attempt to preordain what the "good life" should be for an individual or group of individuals. Instead, the emphasis must surely be on the need for the individual to take *responsibility* for choice one way or another. In practice, this means, in the current context, not opting for a life measured in terms of personal material accumulation and fulfillment of sensual desires (simply because that is what peers and the mass media urge) without serious thought about alternative lifestyles and choices.

In some ways this takes us back to the thinking of virtue ethicists working in the tradition of Aristotle. In this line of thought, ethics is fundamentally about flourishing through the exercise of what is unique in our humanness – our capacity to reason about our most fundamental life-shaping decisions and then choose specific paths which may well differ fundamentally in type from one another. To be fair, not all virtue ethicists would recognize such diversity as inherent in their schema but it is certainly present in the work of a thinker such as David Norton.[18]

This poses a challenge not just to the totalizing tendencies which do exist in the individualist and collectivist approaches but also to current prevailing cultures. Making genuinely individual choices (as Mill acknowledges in the quote above) requires the development of character. Without virtues such as honesty, courage, commitment and temperance, we cannot really make the hard decisions about our lives and stick to the paths they take us down. But this understanding of ethics as well as the value placed on such virtues is hardly a predominant feature of our currently wealth, fame and beauty-obsessed mass media. This ethic implies a degree of serious-mindedness that is somewhat out of fashion in the hedonistic culture that has been created by 30 years of individualism.

At organization level, a culture of diversity and autonomy also needs to operate. Some highly successful companies have embraced this, particularly those operating at the cutting edge of IT. Google is perhaps the best known of these, allowing its employees considerable time to think freely and develop new ideas for the company.

But this ethos needs to extend beyond companies and into all areas of civil society. A notable failure of diversity and autonomy in higher education, for example, is in the field of economics where, over many decades, one particular approach has come to be presented to undergraduates as the only meaningful way to understand an economy. This domination of neoclassical thinking has marginalized a wealth of alternative streams and turned out economists with a narrow and highly contestable understanding of economic reality. This has, in turn, contributed to the shrinking of policy space for governments around the world and has played a major part in the promotion of the constraining individualism that much of this essay has been about.

Maybe the biggest challenge in this regard relates to public services, where a top-down culture often crushes the autonomy of staff and limits the flexibility and diversity of services on offer. The notion, for example, that public service delivery might be free to experiment and diversify more (despite the risk of mistakes being made) is one worth expanding.

Of maybe even greater importance, however, is the need for diversity between organizations. It is this that will allow individuals the freedom to operationalize the serious choices they make about their lives. A society, culture or economy in which the range of organizational options is closed down is the greatest threat to diversity. It is at this point that a possible role for the state emerges as a guarantor of that vital diversity and concomitant freedom.

To take just one historical but topical example: the homogenization of the retail banking sector should immediately have rung alarm bells for any government concerned about diversity. The demutualization of building societies in the 1990s was the removal of a significant (and more collective) option for those seeking banking services. A state which was committed to diversity would have placed restrictions on such activity. Of course, there is a fine judgment to be made sometimes between whether a particular option in an economic sector is disappearing due to lack of consumer interest or due to other factors. But in this case it was clear that members of building societies were effectively being bribed to vote for demutualization and the increased homogeneity of the sector.

And there are still battles to be fought right now over diversity. Charlie Leadbeater has written recently[19] about the major changes afoot on the internet in the form of cloud computing, which will effectively decentralize the internet in ways that will make computer use more efficient and allow access to data from a variety of sources rather than just computers. It is a shift that could well unleash another wave of innovation on the internet. But cloud computing still needs careful management by organized bodies – the question is whether those bodies are homogeneous corporations or whether a greater heterogeneity can be maintained. As Leadbeater says:

> *The first main threat to open cloud culture is homogeneity: we do not want a digital sky dominated by standardised clouds branded Google and Apple. The first principle should be variety: we need public clouds, such as the World Digital Library being created by a set of leading museums around the world and open, social clouds such as Wikipedia.*

This brings us to another role for the state (and other authorities) based on the recognition that the virtues that drive genuine free choice and hence diversity do not appear as if by magic. A base of careful nurturing of children and a continued level of material wellbeing are required for the operation of virtues and the capacity to make real, reasoned choices about one's life. The state cannot provide all that is required by any means but it can certainly go some way to resourcing educational institutions, providing material support to individuals and families, offering healthcare and other crucial services at a level that means that poverty and deprivation do not become a barrier to human growth.

Those who object that such provision acts as a drag on the economy fail to grasp the economic imperatives behind creating a fully educated, healthy and well-resourced population able to act as the innovators and drivers of diversity in the new, increasingly complex markets within which we will have to operate in coming decades.

The notion of a new culture of serious-minded individuals choosing between a wide diversity of options not just as consumers but also as learners, workers, pleasure-seekers and citizens backed by a supportive state which also acts as a guarantor of diversity may sound hopelessly optimistic. But the vision of a world with decent welfare support, free healthcare and secure work, underpinned by a rapidly expanding mass market churning out time-saving and entertaining conveniences to put in new clean, safe homes, seemed far-fetched in the 1930s. Yet this is what had come to pass within 20 years. There was no inevitability about that vision and there is none about this one. All will depend, in the end, on how the opportunities of this new historical turning point are seized.

NOTES

1. See, for example, R. Reeves and P. Collins, *The Liberal Republic*, Demos, 2009.

2. See, for example, J. Cruddas, *The Future of Social Democracy*, Compass, 2010.

3. See, for example, P. Blond, *Red Tory: How Left and Right Have Broken Britain and How we Can Fix It*, Faber & Faber, 2010.

4. A. Goodman, P. Johnson and S. Webb, *Inequality in the UK*, Oxford University Press, 1997.

5. J. Hicks and G. Allen, *A Century of Change*, House of Commons Library, 1999.

6. Office for National Statistics, *Social Trends*, ONS, 2009.

7. The Power Inquiry, *Power to the People*, The Power Inquiry, 2006.

8. A. Lent, *British Social Movements Since 1945*, Palgrave – now Palgrave Macmillan, 2001.

9. M. Brewer, L. Sibieta and L. Wren-Lewis, *Racing Away? Income Inequality and the Evolution of High Incomes*, Institute for Fiscal Studies, n.d.

10. Joseph Rowntree Foundation, *Contemporary Social Evils*, Policy Press, 2009.

11. Hicks and Allen, op. cit.

12. M. Bunting, *Willing Slaves: How the Overwork Culture is Ruining our Lives*, HarperCollins, 2004.

13. S. Lansley, *Unfair to Middling: How Middle Income Britain's Shrinking Wages Fuelled the Crash and Threaten the Recovery*, TUC, 2009.

14. J.S. Mill, *On Liberty*, Longmans, 1965.

15. C. Perez, *Technological Revolutions and Financial Capital*, Edward Elgar, 2003.

16. C. Perez, "The double bubble at the turn of the century", *Cambridge Journal of Economics*, 2009, 33(4): 779–805.

17. C. Leadbeater, *We-think: The Power of Mass Creativity*, Profile Books, 2009.

18. D.L. Norton, *Democracy and Moral Development: A Politics of Virtue*, University of California Press, 1991.

19. C. Leadbeater, *Let's Open Up Cloud Computing, The Guardian* website, 22 January 2010, http://www.guardian.co.uk/commentisfree/2010/jan/22/protect-open-cloud-computing.

6

INVESTMENT BANKING: THE INEVITABLE TRIUMPH OF INCENTIVES OVER ETHICS

John Reynolds

Investment banking is a necessity in the modern economy. It enables companies and governments to finance and carry out increasingly global activities. It offers significant rewards to some investment bankers. It is vulnerable to abuse and the relentless pursuit of money and, by implication, power. Can it be ethical or is it intrinsically unethical, given the huge temptations?

WHY DO INVESTMENT BANKS EXIST?

The modern economy requires investment banks. The role they play includes raising money for governments, transmitting and converting currency around the world, as well as the areas requiring highly specialist advice for companies and governments, which are often prohibitive for all but the largest organizations to retain in-house.

It is helpful to understand the different roles played by and within investment banks. The first crucial separation is between advisory activities and markets. The second is between debt and equity markets. Within markets activities, there is also a clear distinction between those involved in client activities, and those trading on behalf of the investment bank itself. It is also important to note that as well as well-known integrated investment banks, which are active across most areas of investment banking, there are also many firms that specialize in only one activity. In some cases, it can be increasingly difficult to assess the difference between the activities of a division of an investment bank and a hedge fund. This can also be the case in other areas, for example comparing advisory activities with similar services provided by an accountancy firm.

It is also the case that the main drivers of profitability change over time: in the late 1990s, equity issuance was extensive and very profitable. This was again the case in 2009, as banks and financial institutions replenished their balance sheets. At such times, equity research is crucial, and equity analysts have a high profile. During the boom in debt and debt-related products which lasted up until 2007, debt markets and structured financings were a key driver of revenue and profit.

Even in major downturns, there can be successful businesses and divisions, focused on investing in or advising on "distressed" debt.

SUCCESS IN INVESTMENT BANKING: DEFINED BY MAKING MONEY

A successful investment banker will be highly focused on generating revenue and profits for the investment bank – not to the explicit exclusion of ethics, but certainly not focused on ethical issues. Investment banks need to have a framework to ensure ethical issues are not ignored. This can't in practice come from management supervision – deals and trades are too complex and fast moving for management to understand everything that is going on in a large investment bank.

More precisely defining successful investment bankers is not straightforward – investment bankers can carry out a number of different activities – trading, advising, selling, investing. However, investment bankers will judge themselves and judge other investment bankers by their success in generating revenue and profit, and in how much they are paid.

Investment bankers and investment banks will also judge themselves on how they perform in league tables and on corporate profitability and growth – the performance of an investment bank is easily validated. In a large institution, it can be harder to validate the performance of some individual investment bankers – in certain cases, it is clear that an individual is highly successful, in others there are many who will claim a share of the success.

There are some common character traits of a successful investment banker. These will include a high level of focus on their job, a high level of dedication – often forsaking recreational or family-based activities – and often a high level of personal intensity.

MONEY IS CORRUPTING

Investment banks have as their primary purpose making money, and investment bankers are judged on their contribution to this aim. In fact, this is no different in aim to most commercial organizations, but much more open than is normally the case.

Large sums of money can undoubtedly be corrupting. Very few individuals can resist the benefits of wealth – financial security, comfort, power, security for their families. For an individual, the temptation can be too great, and the incentives can make it especially difficult, to forsake short-term financial gain. The ability to earn over £1m in a single year – or approximately 40 times average annual earnings – can change behavior.

For the institution, risk management combined with share ownership, giving an incentive to create equity value (the long-term value of the investment bank), are supposed to provide an incentive to avoid short-term gains at the expense of increased longer term risk. It is a salutary fact that among the large losers from the banking collapse were exactly those people who would have been expected to be motivated to maximize long-term rather than short-term gain – senior investment bankers with a high level of equity ownership in their employers. One of the suggested reforms to investment banking is an increase in using equity (shares) as part of investment bankers' pay, but it is not clear from recent evidence how far this can go to change behavior.

HOW INVESTMENT BANKERS ARE PAID

In investment banks, pay is called "compensation" or "comp" for short. Comp is frequently discussed, and the annual round of determining how a bonus pool is divided is a lengthy and complex process. Most investment banks calculate total comp (basic pay + bonus) for senior investment bankers based on a review of an individual's contribution to the bank's profit or loss. From this perspective, banking can be a true meritocracy. For a banker, a year can be judged on the total compensation received at the year end, which typically comes in a mixture of cash and shares – in general, the higher the amount paid, the higher the proportion of shares.

Most business originators in an investment bank – generally among the most senior investment bankers – whether equity analysts, traders, capital market salespeople or corporate finance advisers, earn a fairly well-understood percentage of the revenue they originate. In a large bank, this may be in the region of 10% of revenue, but can vary significantly depending on a range of factors, such as the seniority of a banker, the policy of the institution itself, prevailing competitive conditions and so on. The percentage will also vary from year to year, depending on the performance of the individual, the department and the overall institution. In a year when everyone does well, payouts would be higher. The reverse can happen in a generally bad year – it can be galling to originate high levels of revenue under these circumstances and then find that it is not rewarded due to poor overall corporate performance.

Although there are market norms, different institutions can have radically different remuneration practices – some giving higher rewards to mid-level bankers, others reserving higher proportions of the bonus pool only for the most senior. In these cases, more junior investment bankers are attracted by the high pay for the small number of investment bankers who successfully reach the top level, even though this inevitably implies a high attrition rate.

One reason for differences in approach among different investment banks to remunerating individual bankers is a significant issue of principle over how much of a banker's revenue is attributable to the banker and how much to the overall institution and therefore its shareholders. This is especially the case with bankers who trade, invest or lend, as their business relies on being given access to the bank's balance sheet and therefore having the investment bank's funds available to them. Varying views can be taken on the value of access to the balance sheet, and the relative contributions of the individuals as opposed to shareholders, who ultimately make the balance sheet available. This can make a major difference to the levels of remuneration paid.

It can be a mistake to focus on how high a "bonus" is paid to investment bankers, for two reasons. First, investment bankers look at their total compensation rather than base salaries. Second, low base salaries derisk the investment bank in a bad year. For example, one mid-sized investment bank pays its equity sales and trading teams purely on the basis of commission and trading profit – a commercially effective strategy, and one which makes the size of a "bonus" a misleading number.

When an investment banker makes a "lateral hire", that is, brings someone in from another investment bank, they will typically agree to pay a guaranteed minimum bonus, especially if the investment banker is relatively senior. Guaranteed bonuses are a complex issue. They can be criticized for reducing the incentive on an individual to work hard and productively, and also for increasing the risk for loyal and long-serving employees of an investment bank. This is because if the institution has a relatively poor year, funds available to pay bonuses are reserved for new employees at the expense of existing employees.

Despite these issues, there are strong reasons why guaranteed bonuses are reasonable, and often necessary. An investment banker, especially at a senior level, will take a period of time to bring in clients and revenue. Typically, this can be in the region of 18 months. As a result, a banker moving employer is at risk of not being fully remunerated for a period of one to two years if there is no guaranteed bonus. Also, investment banking base salaries are anomalously low when compared with peers in the professions or industry. Paying a guaranteed bonus is effectively capital investment by an investment bank, in the same way, for example, that a fast moving consumer goods company will invest in developing and marketing a new brand.

Paying a guarantee is therefore a reasonable risk for an investment bank: a new senior banker is able to be judged based on their performance in another firm, and market reputation is checked through taking detailed references from previous clients, who, it is hoped, will also be future clients. Many corporate clients of successful investment bankers will be at least as loyal to the individual as to the institution.

Over time, bankers can earn significantly more from the equity or shares they receive as part of their compensation package – this increases in value over time if the investment bank is successful, and ties an investment banker into the long-term success of the investment bank.

Investment banks seek to recruit only the brightest and most talented people. In over a decade of taking part in the recruiting process at investment banks, including screening CVs and interviewing as well as discussing conclusions with colleagues, I have never seen or heard of a candidate being rejected because of a concern about too much integrity, although the opposite does happen sometimes and a candidate can be rejected for a perceived lack of integrity.

Hedge funds have an indirect but massive influence on the higher levels of compensation at investment banks. Investment banks have to keep up with market rates of compensation. Hedge funds, which receive base management fees of typically 2% of assets under management, can have a consistent and high basic level of revenue. Consequently, in many cases, they have established higher base levels of compensation than investment banks, and have also, where successful, been able to pay much higher levels of total compensation than received typically by investment bankers. As a result of this, moves to limit pay by regulating investment banks will push more successful traders to less-regulated hedge funds, or other private or offshore investment companies.

EQUITY OWNERSHIP DIDN'T PREVENT INVESTMENT BANKING COLLAPSE

Despite substantial shareholdings being owned by senior executives, some major investment banks collapsed or had to be rescued in 2008–09. The top executives at Bear Stearns and Lehman Brothers suffered substantial losses when the banks collapsed. James Cayne, CEO of Bear Stearns, held 5.6 million shares at the time of the bank's emergency sale to JP Morgan on 25 March 2008,[1] which he sold for $61m. At a peak share price of $171.51,[2] the shares had been worth approaching $1bn. In March 2008,[3] Dick Fuld, CEO of Lehman Brothers, directly and indirectly held 10.9 million shares, which at a peak share price of £85.80, had been worth over $900m. When Lehman filed for bankruptcy on 15 September 2008, those shares became worthless.

Equity ownership is spread broadly in investment banks. As an example, I met a number of Bear Stearns bankers after its collapse, people who were clearly highly competent and had been extremely successful. A number of these investment bankers had at one stage amassed large paper fortunes in the form of equity in their employer – now reduced to virtually nothing. I would not argue that these particular bankers are facing the type of crisis faced by victims of natural disasters, or that they require handouts. Also, Bear Stearns was among the most aggressive of the major investment banks. However, these investment bankers had through hard work made success-ful careers, and had trusted implicitly in the benefit of holding equity in their company – a culture of equity ownership in investment banks has not protected them from financial problems.

CONVERGENCE OF COMMERCIAL BANKING AND INVESTMENT BANKING

The activities of commercial banks – customer accounts, commercial lending, money transmission and so on – are separate to investment banking. However, the two sets of banks have a number of areas of activity in common. This gives rise to obvious opportunities for commercial banks to offer investment banking services – most major banks, such as RBS, HSBC and Barclays, have substantial investment banking businesses as well as retail and commercial banking. In some cases, banks have been fully integrated, in others a commercial bank has offered a small number of niche services.

The cultures of a commercial bank and an investment bank tend to vary greatly, with an investment bank typically encouraging greater entrepreneurialism, although there is no simple benchmark. Traditionally, investment banks sought higher returns for their shareholders than commercial banks, and this divergence clearly narrowed over the past 10–15 years, as commercial banks sought to increase their returns by moving into related areas of investment banking, with the additional effect of increasing their risk profiles.

Various regulations have at times in some countries prevented the convergence of commercial banking and investment banking, notably the Glass-Steagall Act, put in place in the US in 1932 and repealed in 1999 by the Gramm-Leach-Bliley Act. Recently, the Obama administration has announced measures to require the separation of investment banking and commercial banking, and proposed limits on proprietary trading or principal investment. Such measures will inevitably appear artificial in many ways, with relatively arbitrary definitions of "commercial banking" and "investment banking". The more significant effect of the proposals will be to limit the size of individual institutions, thereby reducing the risk faced by governments if bailouts are required in future. In an increasingly global economy, industries with an international footprint – and investment banking is by no means the only one – will be difficult to support when faced with a crisis.

MANAGEMENT

Investment banks can have very different characters and often these persist over a long period of time. Some are more aggressive, others more intellectual. Often, the character and style of an investment bank may be set by a strong chief executive or group of senior managers – this is an industry in which strong characters succeed.

Investment banks are not generally well managed in the sense of traditional man-management – management culture is often more a question of leaving people to work things out and rewarding the successful while at times unceremoniously dumping the unsuccessful. However, investment banks are intrinsically difficult to manage. It is often recognized that it is especially difficult to manage "experts", and organizationally an investment bank consists of groups of such experts. It is even harder to manage people who have become financially independent, as is the case with many senior investment bankers.

In some cases, management strategy can deliberately seek to create tension and stress. The strategies of some investment banks include deliberately creating rivalries between groups, increasing aggressive behavior.

There are problems with the treatment of employees in many institutions, which can lead to short-term behavior. Most bankers, if not all, will have had colleagues who one year were highly productive and relatively shortly afterwards have been redundant for some reason – few investment bankers in my experience will rely on an institution to look after the long-term interests of an individual banker. In particular, junior bankers are often seen as "cannon fodder" when they are hired as graduates. Such junior bankers typically have a high attrition rate over the first two to three years of their careers. This serves to inculcate an intrinsic distrust of the investment bank among investment bankers. In practice, this is one major reason why individual investment bankers may take less care over the long-term implications of their activities than sometimes seems rational, given widespread equity ownership. Another reason for the same approach is the risk that even if one banker is successful, another imprudent trader (or corporate acquisition or strategy) may bring about significant losses, thereby reducing equity value.

In most investment banks, top managers can't be paid an order of magnitude less than their highest paid employees – it is therefore directly in their interest to cultivate highly paid trading strategies.

ABUSE

Investment banking has had high-profile abuses – inappropriate research during the dot-com boom, insider dealing, marketing of high-risk products as low risk. In addition, on a smaller scale, there are other forms of abuse which can take place. There can be a fine line between a practice which is highly innovative, and one which is unethical. It can also at times be difficult to assess how (un)ethical a practice may be if it is new.

It is clear that the potential gains in investment banking will result in some abuse. Just as there are some individual investment bankers who are philanthropic, there are others who are simply greedy and have little or no regard for ethics. More worryingly, I have seen in general less interest from senior management in preventing abuse per se in investment banks than I am comfortable with – if a practice results in profits, it can be easy to let it continue if it does not pose direct risks to the investment bank (that is, it is not criminal, potentially loss-making or in breach of regulatory rules, or, more broadly, a reputational risk).

Two of the major areas of concern in investment banking have been insider dealing – a criminal offence – and short-selling. Both of these are ethically complex. Historically, although insider dealing was for a long time a legitimate practice in many markets, it is now widely covered by criminal law and is in most cases illegal – although in some niche business areas it remains legal. As it is difficult to identify a victim other than "the market" itself, it is logical only to see it as unethical if markets themselves are seen as beneficial or ethical. Short-selling was the subject of significant political concern during the banking crisis, but generally has been regarded as a legitimate market and investment practice.

Insider dealing rules: an example of imperfect regulation

Where there is legislation in place to ensure proper behavior, it is often incomplete, leading to scope for making money out of gaps in the law. One obvious example of this is insider dealing.

Insider dealing is an unusual crime, as it is difficult at times to see who is the victim. However, markets do not work efficiently unless they are fair, and consequently insider dealing is acknowledged to be a real crime. Given this, it is strange that insider dealing rules were not universally applied. They apply to trading of securities on recognized exchanges. Therefore, instruments traded off exchanges can be traded in ways which would otherwise be illegal. Some major investment banks carry out trading activities which are at best ethically unquestionable, but not actually illegal. Such activities have the benefit of extensive legal advice, as the banks concerned would not wish to risk actually breaching securities laws.

Insider dealing is an interesting test of where banks are applying ethical versus legal restrictions to their activities. In my experience, a number of banks will trade securities not covered by insider dealing laws in a way which would apply as insider dealing to relevant securities. This suggests that either the banks concerned do not accept that insider dealing is unethical, but only see it as illegal in some technical way, or alternatively that they fail to consider the ethical issues associated with their activities.

Short-selling: benefiting markets or unethical abuse?

Short-selling is ethically significantly more complex than insider dealing. The practice involves borrowing a share in order to sell it, with an obligation to return a share subsequently. Economically, it is an investment which works if the value of the share goes down rather than up. Shorting is often carried out as part of a "pairs trade". This means that an investor takes a view that company A is overvalued and company B is undervalued, and buys the same value of shares in company B as is sold in company A. This maintains a market neutral position, obviating risks to the investment position associated with general market movements, at the same time as reducing the capital committed to the investment position. If the investor is correct, a high return can be achieved.

The language used to criticize short-selling has included criticism of it as speculation, which can be difficult to define. The nature of "investment" is that it almost certainly involves some level of risk-taking, but can be based on detailed research and is fundamentally supporting economic activity. The nature of gambling is that risk is understood, but returns are by definition subject to random features which cannot be managed or controlled, and is expected to give rise to an undeserved return (undeserved as relating to being based on economic activity). In investment, although any given security would be expected to show stochastic or random volatility and therefore has some of the features of gambling, in principle, over time market valuation should reflect fundamental value.

The actual act of short-selling is no more than selling a share. It is difficult to consider this intrinsically unethical. It is true that short-selling can be abused: it can be used to abusively move market prices; it can be used to facilitate insider dealing; and it can be used to deliberately create distress in a company or for an investor. However, this is no more than the counterpart to the risk of the act of buying shares, which also is potentially subject to abuse.

There is extensive evidence that short-selling leads to increased market liquidity, often viewed by economists and market practitioners as a positive feature. For example, it can assist in preventing investment "bubbles" from materializing. It is a sad fact that when poor investment decisions are made or when companies are poorly run, investors suffer. However, in this context, allowing market mechanisms to expose poor performance or management can assist in preventing greater subsequent losses.

The issue of short-selling can be separated into two ethical issues: selling a share and being in a short position. The act of selling a share is not, in itself, absent some abusive intent, unethical. Equally, being in a position of being "short" is not unethical, and is similar to having borrowed money. This is not to say that shorting cannot be abusive: it is sensible to continue to monitor activity to ensure that none of the possible abuses are being carried out, if lending stock or investing in companies that short-sell. Most if not all major banks in some of their activities either short-sell or facilitate short-selling.

In September 2008, short-selling was seen as a contributing factor to undesirable market volatility in the US and subsequently was prohibited in the US by the Securities and Exchange Commission (SEC). The SEC banned for three weeks short-selling on 799 financial stocks to boost investor confidence and stabilize those companies. In December 2008, SEC Chairman Christopher Cox said the decision to impose the ban on short-selling of financial company stocks was taken reluctantly, but that the view at the time, including from the Treasury secretary and the Federal Reserve chairman, was that "if we did not act and act at that instant, these financial institutions could fail as a result and there would be nothing left to save".[4] Later, Cox questioned the value of these actions. Although the SEC's Office of Economic Analysis was still evaluating data from the temporary ban, and that preliminary findings pointed to several unintended market consequences and side effects, he said:

While the actual effects of this temporary action will not be fully understood for many more months, if not years, knowing what we know now, I believe on balance the Commission would not do it again.[5]

In the UK in October 2009, the Financial Services Authority (FSA) issued a Feedback Statement detailing the responses that the FSA received to its proposals in a February 2009 Discussion Paper on short-selling. This confirmed that the FSA intended to pursue enhanced transparency of short-selling through disclosure of significant short positions in all equities, rather than through a ban. Alexander Justham, FSA director of markets, said:

The consultation exercise has confirmed our support for enhanced disclosure requirements for significant short positions rather than any direct restrictions on short selling, other than on a temporary basis in exceptional market conditions.[6]

COMPLIANCE: LEGALISTIC AND NOT A SUBSTITUTE FOR ETHICS

Compliance is essential in all banks and is designed to ensure "compliance" with all applicable regulation and therefore prevent any abuses. In a narrow and legalistic way, compliance is generally highly effective in investment banks, and few investment bankers would want to breach compliance policy. At the same time, there are two fundamental problems with the culture of compliance. First, the way compliance is implemented in investment banks is normally difficult to take seriously. Compliance can descend into something necessary but often very limited, due to its focus on tick-box exercises. Such an approach is unlikely to work in a broad and meaningful way, given how dynamic markets can be. Second, compliance is very different from ethical thinking.

This is despite the FSA's attempt to focus on principles rather than process, and avoid a mechanistic approach. In April 2007, the FSA published *Principles-based Regulation: Focusing on the Outcomes that Matter*. The 10-point summary stated: "Over the next few years we will move to more principles-based regulation, supplementing our risk-based and evidence-based approach."[7]

The FSA has eleven Principles for Business, which are highly laudable. These include integrity, market conduct and financial prudence.[8] In 2007, the FSA conflated regulation on the basis of principle and self-regulation, shortly ahead of the subprime crisis, which demonstrated a failure in risk controls and self-regulation at major banks and investment banks. This does not mean that regulation based on basic principles is wrong. A principle-based rather than a purely box-ticking approach to regulation is the more effective way to regulate complex international investment banks.

Despite the FSA's principles-based approach, compliance training in investment banks became based on routine tick-box downloads of legally required information in as short a time as possible. In the roughly one hour per year that each investment banker is required to undergo training in compliance, much legally required but generally irrelevant information is disgorged as rapidly as possible, information such as the obligation to know the name of the investment bank's money laundering reporting officer. Much of the information has little relevance to an individual's own responsibility.

I have been involved in a number of substantive discussions of ethical issues, notably in the context of conflicts of interest about whether and how an investment bank could try to relax limits on acting for multiple parties in a single transaction (a practice also sometimes considered by other professional advisers). However, these were not based on compliance training, and were discussed mainly at a senior level. Such discussions were generally not substantive from a real ethical standpoint, so much as aimed at finding how to maximize the potential revenue for the firm.

There have been proposals for a general code of ethics for investment banks in the past, but such an approach is difficult in practice. In part, this is because of the wide variety of different activities carried out by an investment bank. The specific ethical issues associated with proprietary trading or principal investment are very different from those associated with advising clients or publishing research.

Individual investment banks have some type of statement of ethical policy, such as a code of business conduct and ethics. In the main, these look like a combination of general statements of good practice combined with further reinforcement of compliance rules and protection of shareholder interests. Investment bankers rarely consider these codes in their day-to-day activities.

It can be easier for the boards and top management of an investment bank to spend time focusing on ethical issues – but the pressure on individual senior investment bankers is to generate revenue and profits. If ethical thinking is not genuinely pushed down to this level and below, a culture of ethics will not develop in an institution.

Investment banking already has tight standards from a regulatory perspective, especially where customers are concerned. Compliance is already (probably uniformly) rigorously implemented. However, this falls far short of ethical thinking, which is needed in investment banking to protect investment banks themselves as well as customers and counterparties.

ETHICS ARE INTRINSIC IN MARKETS

Is investment banking intrinsically unethical? The capital markets rely on intrinsically ethical behavior: keeping promises – they require the consent of trading counterparties to believe that market bargains will be honored. Markets are generally considered to be beneficial, delivering efficient prices for both buyers and sellers. Also, markets have generally encouraged meritocracy and equality, although I would accept that this is not always the case.

There is extensive discussion over ethics in some investment banks, clearly less so in others. In most cases, although there are discussions over ethics at a senior level, and compliance training at all levels, ethical thinking is not actively encouraged across all levels of investment banks.

With the need for parties to implicitly deal in good faith and accept that their counterparties also deal in good faith, markets intrinsically encourage some forms of ethical behavior. In the end, if a practice is unacceptable to clients or trading counterparties, it tends to be fairly short-lived – probably the best driver of good practice in markets is transparency.

It is notable that many of the now well-known instruments which played a major role in the financial crisis are not traded on recognized exchanges or markets, for example credit default swaps. A faster regulatory response to the development of new instruments and their more rapid incorporation into formal markets is an essential component of increasing transparency and the effectiveness of regulation of investment banking.

Many charities have benefited significantly from the involvement of investment bankers and hedge fund managers, as donors, fundraisers or trustees. Charity fundraising committees, attendance at fundraising events and sponsorship of the arts have all benefited tremendously from investment banking. Some of this has not been selfless, but has had a corporate benefit (sponsorship of the arts); however, a significant amount has simply been philanthropic.

BUBBLES: THE POWER OF BEING RIGHT

One of the ingredients of the banking crisis was a bubble in debt derivatives, notably mortgage-backed securities. Bubbles in themselves are nothing new – they occur frequently across markets. In many ways they are generated even among sophisticated institutions as a successful track record develops. If an investment banker proposes a strategy on a small scale, investing a modest amount of money, and is consistently successful, they will be allocated further capital. As these investment bankers will have been proven successful, it is relatively straightforward for skeptics to be marginalized. After a period of time (which may be a number of years), even the skeptics may be converted by the growing track record and simply assume they were previously wrong. Trading strategies do not have to be based on long-term fundamentals to be correct if they are exercised on a small scale. However, if they become very widespread, it becomes more necessary for their economics to be fundamentally justified. Where the trading or investment strategy is not based on fundamentals, it won't be sustained in the long term.

In a global market, it is probably inevitable that a bubble can become bigger and more dangerous. This does not mean that globalization is bad, but that negative aspects must be recognized and managed.

Although there is no simple and effective way of preventing bubbles, the basic solution is multifaceted and has two principal components: transparency and effective regulation. Just as it is doubtful whether sports players would always follow rules in the absence of a referee, the same is true of investment bankers. Regulation needs to understand investment banking, and to be intelligent. As in the example of insider dealing, rules need to establish a level playing field. This should not, however, restrict the ability to invest or trade based on hard work or detailed analysis.

CONCLUSION

It would be seriously wrong to assume that the nature of investment banking could or should be changed – investment banking works because individuals are focused, motivated and (in the short term) self-sacrificing. Such individuals will be successful not just in investment banking, but in commerce in general.

It is true that there are abuses in investment banking, and some cases are extreme. It is less these rare extreme cases which should be of concern, so much as a generally pervasive culture which actively encourages pushing the law to the limit and going beyond ethical boundaries. Prescriptive legislation and compliance rules will never be able to keep up with the rapid pace of developments in markets and financing – the general culture of investment banking is therefore crucially important.

The financial failure of parts of the investment banking industry following the subprime crisis highlights serious problems within the industry, but not in itself a fundamental failure of ethics so much as a series of gross errors of judgment. At the same time, more rigorous inculcation of ethical thinking at all levels within investment banks would help protect against repeat mistakes based on greed and short-term thinking.

In practice, investment bankers, especially at a senior level, have clear reasons for behaving in line with the law and regulations: first, securities law appears to have become progressively more restrictive, and bankers do not want to be the subject of action by regulators or, worse, criminal prosecution – either of these eventualities can result in a ban in working in the industry; second, investment bankers typically have a meaningful amount of investment in their employer, and have a strong incentive not to prejudice long-term value. The issue is whether these incentives for ethical behavior outweigh the scope for profit from unethical behavior.

The rewards offered can at times be so great that individuals can take significant risks and even knowingly breach ethics and the law. This puts a burden on senior management, themselves subject to the same incentives, and a need for transparency and external regulation. Transparency is crucial – it is much easier for someone without an economic interest to blow the whistle.

Fundamentally, we need investment banks – they provide essential services to support the modern and global economy. The failure of the banking sector came despite huge incentives on senior management to preserve long-term value – the collapse of major investment banks was not in any sense the result of deliberate acts by their management. However, the overwhelming incentive on the individual is typically to make a short-term gain. Management of investment banks has been based on promoting the competent but often without providing training in managing.

Investment banking requires an increased contribution from a combination of management, transparency and regulation. All of these require a contribution from ethics – ethical debate has not often taken the opportunity to engage in complex financial matters. Events since 2007 have shown that the financial world is an integral part of the lives of everyone in the developed world. More transparency and its essential corollary – scrutiny – is essential to allow investment bankers and investment banks to make ethical decisions. Investment banking is not subject to pressure from retail customers, and much of what goes on is not visible externally. Of equal importance, ethics should be a part of the culture of investment banks and pushed down throughout the bank – looking after long-term equity value through behaving ethically should be as thoroughly inculcated into banking culture as looking after clients and shareholders.

NOTES

1. SEC Form 4, http://www.secinfo.com/dNmp6.t1e.htm, accessed 10 May 2010.
2. L.A. Bebchuck, A. Cohenm and H. Spamann, "The wages of failure: executive compensation at Bear Stearns and Lehman 2000-2008", publication forthcoming in the *Yale Journal of Regulation*, http://papers.ssrn.com/sol3/papers.cfm?abstract_id=1513522, accessed 7 January 2010.

3. Proxy statement, http://www.sec.edgar-online.com/lehman-brothers-holdings-inc/def-14a-proxy-statement-definitive/2008/03/05/Section7.aspx, accessed 10 May 2010.

4. A.R. Paley and D.S. Hilzenrath, "SEC chief defends his restraint", *Washington Post,* 24 December 2008, http://www.washingtonpost.com/wp-dyn/content/article/2008/12/23/AR2008122302765.html, accessed 12 January 2010.

5. R. Younglai, "SEC chief has regrets over short-selling ban", 31 December 2008, http://www.reuters.com/article/idUSTRE4BU3FL20081231, accessed 12 January 2010.

6. FSA Feedback Statement, 1 October 2009, http://www.fsa.gov.uk/pages/Library/Communication/PR/2009/131.shtml, accessed 12 January 2010.

7. Financial Services Authority, *Principles-based Regulation: Focusing on the Outcomes that Matter,* April 2007, http://www.fsa.gov.uk/pubs/other/principles.pdf.

8. FSA Handbook, *Principles for Businesses,* PRIN 2.1, http://fsahandbook.info/FSA/html/handbook/PRIN/2/1, accessed 10 December 2009.

7

CULTURE AND THE CRISIS

Andrew Whittaker

INTRODUCTION

My aim in this essay is to look at the specifically cultural issues underlying the recent financial crisis. My theme is that certain cultural trends were highly significant in the emergence of the crisis, and that although these trends are powerful, it is both possible and legitimate to try to change them, and while this may involve action by policy makers, ultimately, cultural change will depend on market participants themselves. I should make plain that this essay does not result from objective research, but from a personal perspective, designed as a stimulus and contribution to a wider debate, and based on my experience as a financial markets lawyer and regulator.

I approach these issues by considering:

- the nature and scale of the financial crisis
- the causes of the financial crisis
- some recent cultural trends in the financial sector
- the impact of these trends on the crisis
- the scope for cultural initiatives
- legitimacy criteria for cultural initiatives
- actual initiatives taken, most particularly by the FSA, but also by the international authorities.

NATURE AND SCALE OF THE CRISIS

The nature and scale of the recent financial crisis are unprecedented. The seminal review by Lord Turner of Ecchinswell, published by the Financial Services Authority (FSA) in March 2009,[1] indicated that

> *over the last 18 months, and with increasing intensity over the last six, the world's financial system has gone through its greatest crisis for at least a century, indeed arguably the greatest crisis in the history of finance capitalism.*

He noted that specific national banking crises had been more severe, but what was unique about this crisis was that

> *severe financial problems have emerged simultaneously in many different countries, and that its economic effect is being felt throughout the world as a result of the increasing interconnectedness of the global economy.*

In his view, it was clear that "however effective the policy response, the economic cost of the financial crisis will be very large".

While recognizing that the crisis has been worldwide in scale, we need also to understand that it is personal in impact. Many people, around the world, are suffering from its effects. It has led to legitimate questioning of causes, and unprecedented policy responses.

CAUSES OF THE CRISIS

The Turner Review sets out to explain what went wrong. In its view, the core of the crisis lay in an interplay between macro-imbalances, which had grown rapidly, and financial market development and innovations. Macro-imbalances arose because large current account surpluses were accumulated by some countries, while large current account deficits emerged in others. A key driver of these imbalances was the very high savings rates in countries like China, whose investors had typically invested in government or government-guaranteed bonds, creating a wall of money which drove a reduction in real risk-free rates of interest to historically low levels. These very low interest rates in turn drove a rapid growth of credit extension in countries like the UK and the US, particularly for residential mortgages, accompanied by a degradation of credit standards, and fueling property price booms, which, for a time, made these lower credit standards appear costless. They also led investors into a ferocious search for yield, so as to gain as much spread as possible above the risk-free rate to offset, at least partially, the declining risk-free rate. The demand for yield uplift, stimulated in this way by macro-imbalances, was met by a wave of financial innovation, focused on securitized debt instruments. This financial innovation sought to satisfy the demand for yield uplift on the basis that, by slicing, structuring and hedging, it was possible to "create value". Securitization of this kind was also seen as a means to reduce banking system risk and to cut the costs of credit intermediation, passing credit risk through to end investors and so reducing the need for expensive bank capital. But when the crisis broke, it became apparent that this diversification of risk holding had not actually been achieved. Instead, most of the holdings, and the vast majority of the losses, were not on the books of end investors, but on the books of highly leveraged banks and bank-like institutions.

In addition to these fundamental causes, the Turner Review deals with more specific issues, under the headings:

- the UK-specific story, of rapid credit growth and significant wholesale and overseas funding
- the problems caused by "global finance without global government", and fault lines in the regulation of cross-border banks
- fundamental theoretical issues about market efficiency and market rationality.

Other inquiries, such as those in the US and the EU, point to similar conclusions.

Regulatory response

Governments and public authorities around the world were and remain keen to respond effectively to the financial crisis. Initial responses focused on managing the crisis as it emerged, by guaranteeing deposits, or providing government support for institutions. A second stage involved action to support growth and jobs, through fiscal expansion, creating a very substantial stimulus to the world economy. So, for example, the G20 committed itself in April 2009 to "deliver the scale of sustained effort necessary to restore growth while ensuring long run fiscal sustainability". A third phase of response is focused on reforming financial systems for the future, with decisions by the G20 to create a new Financial Stability Board, to improve supervision of all significant cross-border financial firms, to improve over time the quality, quantity and international consistency of capital in the banking system, to extend regulatory oversight to limit the risk from gaps in the system, and to endorse common principles on pay and compensation in financial institutions to ensure that these reward actual performance, support sustainable growth, and avoid excessive risk-taking. These actions lie at the heart of what is needed to respond to the crisis. The focus here on cultural issues should not lead us to think otherwise.

CULTURAL TRENDS

But alongside these economic, structural and theoretical causes, and the actions that have been taken to respond to them, it seems to me that it is worth focusing on the cultural trends which may have contributed to the crisis. These are, perhaps, not so different from those causes set out in the Turner Review, but rather a different way of looking at some of them. While a number of these cultural trends are features of society as a whole, I will focus on them specifically as they impacted on the crisis through their place in the financial sector.

In particular, I will focus on three cultural trends in the financial sector under the headings: life in the fast lane – the risk culture; groupthink and the assessment of risk; and the devaluation of values. I will take some time, in the following paragraphs, to say a bit more about what I mean by each of these headings. But some general comments first.

What is the nature of these cultural trends? First, as cultural trends, they reflect the beliefs, decisions and practices of great numbers of people. This gives them a form of legitimacy and a resilience, which are highly significant. Indeed, with some exceptions, they produce their effects as characteristics of a group, rather than of an individual. Second, they are difficult to assess, let alone manage: people may disagree about their existence or importance;

they are not readily measured, but amorphous; not uniform but diverse; not independent of the wider culture of society or the global financial services industry, but permeated by it; not consciously adopted, but developed imperceptibly over time. Third, while particular actions may be morally neutral, collectively, as the characteristics of a group, they can ultimately be highly destructive, for the individuals involved, the wider society, or both.

Turning now to specific trends themselves, I will discuss three cultural trends which seem to me to have been particularly important contributors to the crisis. But I recognize that others may offer a different analysis.

"Life in the fast lane"

The Eagles' 1976 cult song "Life in the fast lane" focused on the traditional pop culture of "sex, drugs and rock and roll". But its title is a good description of a more recent culture of risk-taking. In its most aggressive form, this is about an environment of profit maximization through taking risks, cutting corners, and the elevation of self-interest (or its corporate cousin, "shareholder value") as the highest goal. How did this come to be part of our commercial life?

The way in which people understand their role is significant. One key feature of established investment markets is that they build on the "wisdom of crowds". They do this by bringing together willing buyers and sellers to decide a price at which they are prepared to deal. By turning the interplay of individual self-interest into the public good of an openly established price for an asset, they create a whole that is more than the sum of its parts, helping to justify individual self-interest, however aggressive, as a moral imperative or at least creating a quasi-moral justification for it.

The effect of this underlying understanding has been reinforced by changes in business structures and methods. "Big Bang" started the process in 1986, with changes in ownership from a partnership to a corporate model, and the growth of the City as a successful wholesale market based both on relationships and on common awareness of the need for buyers to beware. Over the years, customer business has moved from a focus on relationships to a focus on deals. Profitability, and so power within institutions, has changed, moving away from bankers or brokers with an ongoing relationship to dealing by professional and proprietary traders. This move away from relationships has in turn reduced societal safeguards and divorced profitability from the market discipline of showing value-added. If you will never see your counterparty again, perhaps never even know who they are, you are unlikely to care whether they feel good about a transaction they have done with you. And of course, if your counterparty is an intermediary too, incentivized only to do deals, rather than build relationships of confidence and trust, progressively the market as a whole will focus more on short-term rather than long-term benefits, on a bottom line divorced from the interests of end users.

A third factor is a bonus culture. Large performance-based incentives, based on performance in a single year, and with no clawback if positions turn bad, undoubtedly led to the build-up of huge risk positions within many institutions, "toxic assets" which, when risks crystallized, undermined confidence in the soundness of the institutions themselves. The pressure such incentives create for rent extraction, taking as much as you can out of your client or your overall position in the market, is probably also at the root of much informed public concern about the bonus system.

"Groupthink" and the assessment of risk

Within this highly pressured environment, as elsewhere, we can see issues of groupthink. The idea of "groupthink" is a well-understood cultural phenomenon. Groups of people tend to think in the same way, whether or not they are members of a formal belief system. Individuals within the group tend to adopt the dominant views of the group. Individuals who stand out against the views of the group are the exception rather than the norm. The group typically rejects challenge to its views, and sometimes the challenger too. Groupthink can be fostered by mutual interests, by a common environment, or even by management or regulatory initiatives.

So a common approach to measuring risk can focus attention on measuring risks in a particular way, rather than in other ways which may convey equally valid truths about their nature. The standard methodologies of regulators, accounting standard setters and rating agencies, however necessary they are, inevitably bring about a degree of groupthink, and discourage alternative ways of viewing situations. This both blinds the group to alternative ways of seeing things, and allows advantage to be taken by those who manipulate standard methodologies in order to disguise risk.

Alongside this is a tendency to favor "propositional knowledge", the kind you can express in the form of a clear, logical proposition, over equally valid evaluative knowledge, which requires the exercise of judgment and understanding to see its force. Good "systems and controls", or the management information they provide, can divert attention from underlying realities and provide a convenient displacement activity for people who would otherwise be forced to focus on uncomfortable or unnerving truths.

But the cultural concerns about standardized risk management and capital approaches go further. They focus too on the reliance that is placed on them. For the foreseeable future at least, standardized systems will always deal poorly with "black swans". You may remember the story, recalled in Nassim Nicholas Taleb's book,[2] about the discovery of the first black swan. Until the discovery of Australia, everyone believed that all swans were white. All the evidence pointed that way. Across the whole known world there had never been a single black swan. There was no basis to conclude that there could be. The chances of one emerging would have been regarded, on the basis of evidence, as infinitesimal. But when Australia was discovered, it became apparent that there could indeed be black swans in considerable numbers. So in the financial system, risks are measured by projections from past experience. The projections may be perfectly valid as projections of existing trends. They may be stress tested against the effects of past downturns or crises. But they will always be poor predictors of the rare and unexpected event.

The devaluation of "values"

"Values", the sense of right and wrong, the sense that there are things that are more important than making money on an individual transaction, can become devalued in an environment or system that is focused on money, or performance measured in terms of money. Value boundaries are undermined by pressure to innovate and be seen as "up for it". There is an insidious pressure to bend the rules, to focus on appearance and how things can be presented to appear to comply with them. Increasing specialization allows responsibility for "compliance" or risk to be laid off on others, or shared with them in obscure ways which seem to allow everyone to avoid responsibility for ultimate outcomes. Personal accountability is undermined, but alongside this, "success" breeds a "star culture", reflecting the celebrity culture of wider society. And all this is understandable. It is at least part of the culture of the financial industry worldwide. It is the culture of many Western societies. Ethics is relegated to the personal sphere, or to a purely nominal allegiance to a set of "corporate values", with organizational culture often focused, in reality, on the dominant duties to shareholders, the tyranny of the bottom line.

In parallel, the state – government and public authorities in many areas – has tended to move into the ethical area. This has not so far played a major part in wholesale market regulation, which has tended to give too much – or rather, the wrong – weight to ideas of "buyer beware" and "the market is always right". Where regulation or law has been set out for these markets, it has focused on clearly defined requirements, like the duty to obtain the market price for a consumer, rather than issues of judgment. But we need to recognize that there has been a huge growth of financial market law, which can drive out moral standards. On this view, the standards that matter are those that are written down on behalf of the authorities, rather than those adopted by individuals or communities. Values that go beyond strict requirements are seen as luxuries, whose sphere, if any, is to inform the private choices of the individual, rather than actions in the commercial or public arena. Action becomes acceptable if you can get away with it. The minimum standard becomes the common standard. We need to be at least alive to the possibility that the progressive incorporation of ethical standards into legal or regulatory requirements not only reflects but legitimizes the marginalization of values or standards which are not reinforced in this way. Further, it changes the "nature" of the standards. From being freely adopted, they become imposed; from being informal, they become formal; from being enforced only by the community, they become enforced by the organs of the state: in fact, from being ethics, they become law.

None of this is to suggest that the law should have no moral or ethical content, or that ethics should never be reinforced by law. It is simply to recognize that this is part of a process which accompanies, even if it does not form part of, a marginalization of those values which go beyond what the law requires. And it is a process that can have real costs in undermining the wider perceptions of value or right and wrong which ought to inform our decision-taking.

IMPACT OF THESE TRENDS ON THE CRISIS

In terms of the build-up of risk, it is easy to see how a culture which fosters risk-taking can lead to a build-up of risk. At the heart of this has been the "originate and distribute" model. Under this, a bank can lend ("originate") in the expectation that it will be able to package up the income stream from its loans into securities which can then be sold to end investors. As is now well known, this led to a willingness to lend to poor credit risks, secure in the belief that any ultimate loss would be borne by an end investor, rather than by the lender. Free from the capital charges which would have applied if they had kept the loans on their own books, lending banks were able to repeat the process multiple times. In turn, this cheap and widely available credit caused an asset price boom, with house prices in particular kept at unsustainable levels by the demand created. As described in the Turner Review (p. 25):

> *the securitized credit model described above, operating within the context of a sustained period of strong global growth, low inflation and a reduced macro-economic volatility, played a major role in stimulating a self-reinforcing cycle of falling risk aversion and rising irrational exuberance of the sort to which all liquid traded markets are at times susceptible. They also created a system which, when confidence broke, and risk aversion rose, was highly susceptible to a self-reinforcing cycle of deleveraging, falling asset prices, and collapsing liquidity.*

As a comment about a business model, we need to be wary of a direct read-across to a conclusion about culture. But we can see how a business model which encourages risk-taking, free from the consequences of the risk, can also support a culture of risk-taking. And it is also apparent how this can be fostered by the other trends we have identified – groupthink and the devaluation of values.

SCOPE FOR CULTURAL INITIATIVES

The challenge, then, is that these facets of industry culture seem to have helped to produce a huge financial crisis. Further, aside from these economic dangers, with their human costs, they may be damaging to the human potential of market participants, let alone the society they serve. Is there then scope to change these apparently dangerous and destructive cultural trends?

If we wish to do so, we can expect the way ahead to be hard. A cultural trend can be widespread and very resilient. It may have evolved progressively through the decisions of thousands of individuals. It provides a motivating power for its participants. It may have a cultural derivation from a wider global culture and roots in UK and Western culture generally. And, although you would expect the recent financial crisis to have had a chastening effect, my impression is that this culture has not so far proved to be self-regulating, not really adapted to reflect how near we came to disaster. Rather, the emphasis has been on the need to go back to "business as usual". Perhaps this is just a sign that cultural change is inevitably slow. Perhaps it is because of the difficulty of identifying alternatives. Perhaps it is because of deep roots in the culture of society. Or perhaps it is about the uncertain impact of the available tools for changing culture, even for an institution which wished to do so.

In the same way, any attempt by the public authorities to tackle issues of culture faces the same problems, and, operating at one remove, clearly risks creating something worse, perhaps just a time-wasting bureaucratic substitute for a genuinely improved culture, but perhaps even a culture with new and unpredictable failings. Nevertheless, no culture is inevitable. Collectively, we are free to change aspects of our culture, if we wish. And, at least potentially, cultural change can be encouraged or discouraged by incentives. Moderating the incentives created by a bonus structure should be just as capable of moderating a bonus culture as increasing them can encourage it.

THE LEGITIMACY OF CULTURAL INITIATIVES

Even if changing elements of the current culture were possible and desirable, would it be legitimate? Is it right for public authorities to try to change a culture, apparently freely adopted? It sounds arrogant, undemocratic even, for a public authority to take action to try to change a culture. However, I would suggest that it *may* be legitimate, under particular conditions.

Much has been written about the principles of good (or "better") regulation. The underlying requirement is that it should be done fairly, or justly. In this context, I would suggest the following principles, some of which are loosely derived from the ancient principles of the "just war":

- the action is necessary to achieving a *legitimate objective*, properly endorsed by a lawful and democratic mandate
- it places a high value of *freedom of choice*, so long as others are not put at risk, preferring a "nudge" over a requirement
- it is done *overtly and directly*, not covertly or through manipulation
- it is done by *lawful means*, in a way that is *proportionate and fair*
- there is a *reasonable prospect of success* which justifies the costs and risks involved.

These criteria are, perhaps, no different from those which apply to any regulatory initiative. With the caveats we have seen about the scope for cultural initiatives, which should always lead to a reluctance to intervene, they apply in the same way.

So if these conditions can genuinely be met, it is, in my view, clear that it can be legitimate for public authorities to aim to influence culture, using drivers of culture for which they are responsible, to avoid creating damaging cultures, to limit the damage caused by existing cultures and to help create new cultures. But there are still fundamental problems. The first is how much confidence you can have that these criteria are met in a given case. The second is that, like the criteria for a just war on which, in part, they are based, much will depend on who is assessing the criteria, and in particular on their motivations, incentives and good judgment.

We also need to recognize that the existing culture has itself been fostered and incentivized by action by governments and regulators. The issue is not whether governments and public authorities should influence culture. They inevitably do, for good or ill. The issues are whether they should do so consciously and deliberately, and whether they should do so with cultural *change* as an aim, rather than simply to go with the grain of an existing culture.

Examples of cultural initiatives over the years

So while we may consider that it is legitimate for public authorities to embark on cultural initiatives, and that if the aim is to change behavior, this will often be an important way to try to do so, the difficulties outlined above suggest that this should be done on a clearly focused and targeted basis. Indeed, that is the approach which financial regulators have taken over the years, when they have tried to tackle cultural issues. So, it is worth considering a few initiatives of this kind in the past, before the recent financial crisis, as well as some aspects of the post-crisis response which have targeted these issues.

Early work by the FSA considered a range of issues on ethics, ultimately concluding that it was right to maintain a clear distinction between regulatory requirements and ethical standards, but that this allowed for the inclusion of some ethical concepts within regulatory standards. So when the FSA introduced a statement of 11 principles (based on a set of 10 published in 1992 by the Securities and Investments Board), it pitched them deliberately with a moral content, designed to reinforce ethical standards and good practice. These principles, like a kind of "11 commandments" for the financial services industry, include provisions which require a firm to "conduct its business with integrity", "observe proper standards of market conduct" and "pay due regard to the interest of its customers and treat them fairly".[3]

Another cultural initiative undertaken by the FSA was focused on the principle of "treating customers fairly". Although much criticized for the bureaucratic approach it engendered, the aim of this treating customers fairly initiative was specifically to change the culture within retail investment firms to place more emphasis, at every stage, on the embedding of the need to ensure that customers were treated fairly. This was very much seen as a cultural initiative, starting with senior management, rather than about systems and controls and processes. Results from the program have suggested that it has made an impact, but the environment has also changed considerably since its inception, and its long-term impact remains to be assessed.

POST-CRISIS INITIATIVES

Following the financial crisis, action has been taken on culture-type issues in three areas. The first is concerned with remuneration structures and their impact on risk, the second with corporate governance, and the third with the skills of individuals with significant influence in firms.

The role of financial regulators in relation to remuneration within the financial services industry arises in three areas. The first is primarily about the structure rather than the amount of remuneration, and focuses on its impact on risk-taking and the risk culture. The second is about the overall quantum of remuneration, and the impact it has on the financial condition of the firm. In particular, can firms which need to rebuild their capital really afford to pay out the large sums by way of remuneration for their staff (or indeed their shareholders) which markets seem to demand? The third is about the overall economic cost of intermediation. In particular, whether the institutional market power and pressure for rent extraction mean that the financial system is taking more out of the economy than it should. These comments focus on the first of these, and the way in which the financial regulators have sought to reduce the incentivization of risk-taking involved in the annual bonus process. The main route has been through the decision by the G20 to endorse the Financial Stability Forum's common principles on pay and compensation in financial institutions.[4] These are designed to ensure compensation structures reward actual performance, support sustainable growth and avoid excessive risk-taking. In particular, they provide for bonus distributions to be partly withheld, and subject to clawback (p. 14), if positions believed to be profitable turn out not to have been so. The UK is the first country to have implemented these proposals, and is still in the course of doing so. While they do not address the public disquiet about the size of remuneration in the financial sector, they should help to address the one-sided incentives which bonuses can create and the risk-taking culture they engender.

In terms of corporate governance, Sir David Walker's report in November 2009[5] was clear that "corporate governance failures contributed materially to excessive risk taking and to the breadth and depth of the crisis". It was equally clear that successful reform depended on *behavioral* change of a kind which it is reasonable to link to some of the cultural trends discussed here. As he saw it, the overriding strategic objective of a bank or other financial institution should be the successful management of financial risk. Achieving this would require a combination of financial industry experience and independence of mind. He saw the FSA's approved persons regime as the mechanism by which the quality of boards should be assessed against these criteria. In addition, he proposed structural changes to the way banking and financial institutions govern themselves, encouraging the use of risk committees separate from audit committees, and made a series of proposals about incentive payments, which he recommended should be incorporated into the FSA code of practice on remuneration in 2010.

Would it be fair to characterize these proposals as aimed at cultural change? In my view "yes". Although they do not refer to cultural change, their success is expressly recognized to be dependent on behavioral change. They focus on incentive structures, and risk management in a way that can be seen as tackling the extremes of the bonus culture. And they have a strong people agenda, with their stress on the importance of financial industry experience and independence of mind.

In parallel with the Walker Review, and consistent with its recommendations, the FSA has adopted a much more intrusive approach to the approval of all individuals, but particularly those who will exercise the most senior roles in high-impact banks and financial institutions. So, for the first time, candidates to occupy the key roles in these institutions are likely to be interviewed by the FSA, to check their suitability, even though the responsibility for selection will remain with the prospective employer. Experience of this new process to date suggests that perhaps 10%

of applications are withdrawn at the interview stage. Four hundred interviews are expected in the course of 2010, and the FSA has recruited a high-level panel of FTSE 100 executives to advise its decision takers in testing the competence and capacity of candidates.

In its January 2010 consultation paper,[6] the FSA made clear that in applying the "fit and proper" test for approval of individuals, exercising roles with significant influence in high-impact (that is, large) firms, it would assess only issues in which it had a regulatory interest (pp. 11ff.). But it made plain that this would include the individual's ability to play their role in delivering effective governance, and their willingness to work with the regulator in an open and cooperative way. The paper also makes clear that, in evaluating the quality of governance, the FSA will look closely at, among other things, "the key factors, such as incentives and culture, which support and enable robust governance" (p. 34).

CONCLUSIONS

It is hard for conclusions in such a wide-ranging area to be definitive. While the causes of the financial crisis were largely economic and structural, a good case can be made for the role of cultural issues. It is both possible and legitimate for policy makers to try to tackle such cultural issues, but also difficult and risky. But on a targeted basis, it is consistent with what regulators have done in the past, already part of the response to the crisis, through action on bonuses, governance and individual fitness. The challenge, perhaps, as we rebuild the world's financial and regulatory systems, is to recognize the importance of people issues, alongside economic and structural ones, and to ask how better we can identify risks inherent in cultures. These are tasks that cannot be achieved by policy makers alone, but is down to all of us, particularly those of us working in the financial system, to see and understand the cultural dynamics within which we are operating, and to identify the challenges they potentially raise for us all.

NOTES

1. *The Turner Review: A Regulatory Response to the Global Banking Crisis*, FSA, 18 March 2009, http://www.fsa.gov.uk/Pages/Library/Corporate/turner/index.shtml.

2. N.N. Taleb, *The Black Swan: The Impact of the Highly Improbable*, Allen Lane, 2007.

3. *FSA Handbook*, http://fsahandbook.info/FSA/html/handbook/PRIN/2/1.

4. Financial Stability Forum, *FSF Principles for Sound Compensation Practices*, http://www.financialstabilityboard.org/publications/r_0904b.pdf.

5. Walker Review, *A Review of Corporate Governance in UK Banks and other Financial Industry Entities: Final Recommendations*, HM Treasury, 26 November 2009, http://www.hm-treasury.gov.uk/d/walker_review_261109.pdf.

6. FSA, *Effective Corporate Governance*, http://www.fsa.gov.uk/pubs/cp/cp10_03.pdf.

8

RECONCILING THE MARKET WITH THE ENVIRONMENT

Zac Goldsmith

There can be no doubt at all that the natural world, on which we all depend for each and every one of our needs, is in serious trouble. Yes, we can argue about aspects of climate science, and, yes, we can quibble with some of the predictions. After all, there is no computer model in the world that can truly take into account the full complexity of ecological systems. But the looming environmental crisis is a basic observation, not a theory.

In 2005, the UN conducted a wide-ranging audit of the planet's health.[1] Its conclusions were stark. It reported:

Over the past fifty years, humans have changed ecosystems more rapidly and extensively than in any comparable period of time in human history, largely to meet rapidly growing demands for food, fresh water, timber, fibre and fuel. This has resulted in a substantial and largely irreversible loss in the diversity of life on Earth.

Its findings make for sobering reading. Between 1970 and 2003, the population of land species declined by nearly a third. Populations of tropical species declined by more than half over the same period. In the past 30 years, humanity has destroyed almost half the planet's original forests.

We are altering the very systems upon which we depend. Without coral reefs and mangroves to act as "fish nurseries", fish stocks simply collapse. Without certain species of bee or wasp, many plants cannot be pollinated and will not grow. Without rainforests, the planet loses not only thousands of as-yet-undiscovered species, but also a "carbon sink" that helps to slow climate change.

At the root of all this is some simple mathematics. The human population is growing, along with our hunger for resources – but the Earth itself isn't. It's an uncomfortable fact, but it is nevertheless inescapable. Oil will eventually run out, and what remains is in the hands of countries we can't always rely on. The world's great breadbaskets are shrinking at an alarming rate, and water shortages now affect more than 100 countries. All this, and there remains the biggest environmental challenge of all – climate change.

What was once a marginal scientific debate has become the framing argument for all our discussions about the future. If even the most conservative predictions are accurate, the effects will be serious – just how serious depends on how fast we act now to stave off the worst of its effects. When an organization like Red Cross International warns that aid will not be able to keep pace with the impacts of climate change, we should be concerned, and still more so when major financial institutions issue similar warnings.

According to German reinsurers Munich Re,[2] the economic losses from natural disasters increased eightfold from the 1960s to the 1990s. About 80% of this resulted from extreme weather-related events. The company now predicts that, by 2065, damages will outstrip global assets. The United Nations Environment Programme's insurers believe that worldwide losses linked specifically to climate change will reach a yearly $304bn in 50 years' time. It is the insurance industry's function to put a price on danger. Their warnings cannot simply be brushed aside.

In his report to the British government in 2006, World Bank economist Nicholas Stern described climate change's potential for major economic disruption and social chaos.[3] The cost of delaying action, he said, is far greater than we can accommodate, and the longer we delay, the higher those costs will be.

But while climate change is the biggest problem we face, it is a symptom of our dysfunctional relationship with the planet. Even if we deny the existence of climate change, we would still need to address the fact that our water consumption globally is growing at twice the rate of our population. We would still need to recognize the importance of food security as breadbaskets become deserts, water tables fall and our own farm base dwindles. We would still need to address the fact that we are dependent for our every need on oil – a finite resource to which access can never be guaranteed. We would still need to prevent the destruction of forests, coral reefs, wilderness areas and the species which depend on them.

In other words, we would still have a big problem on our hands. And we would still need to act swiftly and with determination to prevent it from getting worse.

It is often hard to reconcile the relentless horror stories with the reality of Britain today: a reality in which life, for many people, is materially better than it has ever been. Two centuries of industrialization and economic growth have brought huge material progress. We have better homes, jobs, education and healthcare than ever before. We can fly to any nation in the world in a matter of hours. The internet can find us almost anything at the click of a mouse.

But the global economy does a good job of hiding its consequences. It is a hugely effective system for delivering immediate wealth, but it cannot possibly deliver the same wealth to future generations. Our economy grows at the expense of the natural world; its fresh water, forests, hydrocarbons, fisheries and farmland. The effect is that almost none of the wealth it creates can be transferred to our children. We know that we cannot continue to consume the world's resources at the rate we are without expecting them to run out at some point. But that very basic truth has almost no bearing on policy decisions.

There comes a moment where the news is so bleak that people are inclined to throw their arms in the air and simply give up. Faced with a barrage of bad news in relation to the global environment, people increasingly ask: "what's the point?" Even if Britain magically gets its act together, they say, what difference can that possibly make if other countries do not follow? But while the problems are indeed vast, they are not insurmountable. Solutions exist, relatively straightforward, even painless ones. But they need to be on the same scale as the problems.

We cannot, for instance, simply "green consume" our way to sustainability. We can buy energy-efficient light bulbs and organic food; we can invest our money ethically, and growing numbers of people do. All this is good news – but for this to make a real difference, they would need to be taken up by everyone, and realistically that just isn't going to happen in time.

It's not that people are uninterested in being part of the solution. Virtually every opinion poll on the subject shows that the majority of people genuinely value the natural environment. Time and again they express strong views on tackling climate change, protecting local landscapes and living sustainably. The trouble is, most green choices cost more. If you want to be environmentally friendly – drive a green car, take the train or eat good quality local food – the cost can be prohibitive. For many people, it's just not a realistic option.

It is government leadership that will be the difference between success and failure. Unless pollution and the use of scarce resources become a direct financial liability, we have no realistic chance of shifting to a clean economy. Politicians know this. The environment has never been so high on the political agenda. It has moved from being the preserve of professional environmental organizations to the public sphere. Global businesses like BP, Shell and HSBC write open letters to the prime minister calling for greater clarity on climate change policies. But few politicians are prepared to take the necessary action. Nothing happens. Time ticks by, the situation grows more urgent – and government does nothing. Why?

The answer is fear. Politicians are terrified of acting because they believe that tackling the looming crisis will involve restricting people's lives. They believe that saving the planet means inhibiting the economy, and that neither business nor voters will stand for it. They fear the headlines of a hostile media. They fear, ultimately, for their careers. It always seems easier to do nothing – to let the situation drift and hope that someone else takes the risk.

In the context of a recession that has cost many people their jobs, their savings and even their homes, the decisions appear harder still. Meanwhile, critics of the environmental agenda claim that the cost of a green economy would be hundreds of billions, if not trillions, of pounds. However, they confuse cost with investment. For example, if I invest 100 units in improving the energy efficiency of my local school, and save 20 units each year thereafter as a result, that represents a hugely rewarding investment opportunity. And the shift doesn't require "new" money. There would be no need for net tax increases to pay for our indulgence in things green. It simply requires bullish signals from government. If a cost is attached to pollution and waste, businesses will minimize both. And if the funds raised from taxing these activities are used to incentivize the alternatives, we will see a dramatic shift in the movement of money towards the kinds of investments and activities that we need.

With the right encouragements, whole sectors could change their investment strategy. UK pension funds, for instance, control about £860bn. Imagine the impact if they chose to invest it in the new green economy? The necessary changes do not need to be painful. The right environmental solutions would help, not hinder, people struggling to cope. And when we emerge from the recession, as we know we will, we can do so with an economy that is environmentally literate, where green choices that are currently available only to the wealthy become available to all. And what makes it easier is that almost everything that needs doing is already being done somewhere in the world. If we took the best of today in every sector and made it the norm tomorrow, we'd already be halfway there or further.

One of the most inspiring examples of a company blazing a trail is Interface, the giant US carpet company. Modern carpeting is hugely wasteful. It lasts on the floor for an average of 12 years, and then spends 20,000 or more years in landfill. In 1996, Ray Anderson, the company's director, asked his staff to work out the company's ecological footprint. He was staggered to learn that 1.2 billion pounds of raw materials had been extracted to produce the $800m worth of carpets sold by the company the year before. Shocked, Anderson decided to rethink the business model completely. Instead of simply selling carpet, the company now sells a "carpet service". Customers pay a monthly fee for a service that guarantees permanently fresh-looking carpets. As the carpet tiles wear out, they are replaced by the company and recycled. The effect is that clients always have good quality carpets, and the company has a clear incentive to make carpets that last.

Since the initiative was introduced in 1995, the company has diverted a mass of more than 100 million pounds of material away from landfill. The energy used to produce the carpets is down 41%, the equivalent of 61,000 barrels of oil. Emissions reductions are down 56%, the equivalent of taking 21,000 cars off the road for a year, and water use is down 73%. And, crucially, the initiative has saved the company $316m through eliminating waste. Meanwhile, Interface has expanded to become the world's largest seller of modular carpet tiles.

Governments too have taken the initiative. In an effort to boost the microgeneration of energy, the German government, for example, has introduced a mechanism for rewarding homeowners for generating their own energy, called the "feed-in tariff". Anyone generating photovoltaic solar power, wind power or hydroelectricity is guaranteed a 20-year fixed payment at a level designed to cut payback time to a matter of years. It has given industry the certainty of long-term demand to make it worthwhile investing in new technologies and generating plants. The results have been spectacular. Germany has 200 times as much solar energy as Britain. It generates 12% of its electricity from renewables, compared with 4.6% in Britain. The industry has also created a quarter of a million jobs – a number that is growing fast. In stark contrast, Britain has only 25,000, the same number as Germany created in 2008 alone. However, feed-in tariffs were introduced in the UK on 1 April 2010.

Another area that has been successfully addressed at the national level is marine destruction. In just a few decades, we have brought the world's oceans to the brink of exhaustion. Between 70 and 80% of the world's marine fish stocks are either fully exploited, overexploited, depleted or recovering from depletion. Fifteen of the seventeen largest fisheries in the world are so heavily depleted that future catches cannot be guaranteed. This is more than an environmental issue. About 200 million people depend directly on the fishing industry. For more than a billion people, fish is their primary source of protein.

But some regions are bucking the trend by establishing marine protected areas where fishing is prohibited. In the Leigh Marine Reserve, New Zealand, established in 1975, the most common predatory fish are six times more abundant in the reserve than outside. In the same country's Tawharanui Marine Reserve, protected since 1981, there are 60% more species in the reserve than outside. Meanwhile, in Spain, which has suffered horribly from overfishing, catches close to the Tabarca Marine Reserve, created in 1986, were 50–85% higher after six years of protection than elsewhere. In the Galician fishing village of Lira, Spanish fishermen are now campaigning for a local reserve of their own – the first time this has ever happened.

Finally, Better Place, a California-based start-up company backed by the Israeli and Danish governments, is finding ways to mainstream electric cars. Better Place essentially offers a "battery service" much like a mobile phone contract. Consumers do not buy batteries. They buy into a contract that allows them to swap their depleted battery with freshly charged ones at any one of a large number of battery stations. The cost of driving is dramatically reduced, and all the reasons we wouldn't normally buy an electric powered vehicle (not least fear of being stranded) are removed.

Where companies, communities and even governments have done the right thing, they have been rewarded for it. Genuine solutions are there, and they work.

Politicians need to understand that reconciling the market with the environment is our defining challenge. And that it is possible. By shifting taxes, removing perverse subsidies and creating clear signals, the shift will happen naturally. Government can use the legislative process to encourage good behavior and discourage bad. It can harness the power of the market, and work with business to retool society for a greener age. Opportunities will spring up, jobs will be created and we will enjoy the emergence of a sustainable, constant economy.

The trouble is, when politicians do promise action, they often pick the wrong solutions. They are either superficial attempts to grab headlines, or clumsy, unpopular measures that give green politics a bad name. If a government is serious about the risks of climate change, it doesn't build homes on flood plains. If it is genuinely concerned about the growth in emissions from aviation, it shouldn't plan to treble airport capacity. If it knows that 15 of the world's 17 fisheries are at the point of collapse, it shouldn't make policy as if those stocks are healthy and will last forever. If it wants to change consumer behavior, it wouldn't adopt clumsy, so-called "green taxes" that do little but anger consumers and businesses alike.

The task is to marry the environment with the market. We need to reform those elements of our economy that encourage us to damage, rather than nurture, the natural environment. In other words, we need a revised approach to market economics that takes the planet into account. The great strength of the market is its unique ability to meet the economic needs of citizens. Its weakness is that it is blind to the value of the environment. Unrestrained, we will fish until the seas are exhausted, drill until there is no more oil and pollute until the planet is destroyed.

But other than nature itself, the market is also the most powerful force for change that we have. A mechanism must be developed that will price the environment into our accounting system: to do business as if the Earth mattered, and to make it matter not just as a moral choice but as a business imperative. Destruction of the natural environment has to become a liability, not an externality. We shouldn't have to choose between the economy and the biosphere. We need to merge them. That means rejecting growth based on environmental degradation, and rigorously applying the principle of making the polluter pay. This is a fundamental principle. Put into practice, it would rapidly change the economy. Polluting companies would be at an economic disadvantage, while clean ones would be favored by the market.

Today, the opposite is more likely. Dirty companies can offload the costs of their pollution onto the taxpayer, and regularly do. For example, we spend about £300m each year cleaning pesticides out of our drinking water. Worse, global taxpayer subsidies to fossil fuels worldwide are estimated to be in the region of $300bn each year. Each year the British government spends £750m propping up fossil fuel projects throughout the world via the Export Credit Agency.

So what specifically needs to be done to reframe the way markets work? First, we need to use market-based instruments such as taxation. When these tools cannot work, we need to change the boundaries within which the market functions by using well-targeted regulation.

Taxation is the best mechanism for pricing pollution and the use of scarce resources. If tax emphasis shifts from good things like employment to bad things like pollution, companies will necessarily begin designing waste and pollution out of the way they operate. Green taxation is about triggering a shift to a cleaner way of doing things. To be effective, it needs to incentivize the right behavior through tax breaks, and that needs to be paid for by taxing polluting behavior.

But people do not trust governments, so it's crucial that whatever money is raised on the back of taxing "bad" activities is seen to be used to subsidize desirable activities. Green taxation should never be retrospective, it should be revenue neutral for governments, and it needs to be totally transparent.

Take cars for example. There are 34 million registered vehicles on our roads today. Roughly 28 million of them are cars, and that number is growing. Instead of adding new "pollution" taxes to existing cars, effectively punishing people for decisions that have already been made, the government should be encouraging change at the point where it matters – at the point of purchase. To trigger a rapid shift in the quality of our cars, the government should introduce a significant "purchase tax" on the dirtiest cars and, crucially, match it pound for pound with tax relief on the cleanest cars.

Green taxes have already earned a bad name in the UK, principally because wherever they have been introduced, they have been retrospective and set at levels that wouldn't realistically change behavior. And because the proceeds have not ostensibly been earmarked to subsidize green alternatives, they have rightly been seen as stealth taxes. A rare example of a green tax that both worked and was accepted by the public is the 1996 landfill tax, which immediately transformed waste into a liability. The proceeds of the tax were initially reinvested into communities affected by landfill sites.

The other major tool in the policy makers' kit is trading. Carbon emissions trading is a good example of a market-based approach which attaches a value to carbon emissions and ensures that buyers and sellers are exposed to the price. As long as the price is high enough to influence decisions, it can work, as the environmental and economic costs of carbon emissions are then directly translated into financial liabilities.

The European Union Emission Trading Scheme (ETS) is the largest "cap and trade" system in the world. EU governments agree a cap on emissions for different sectors of the economy within each EU country. Carbon quotas are then allocated by those countries to individual businesses. The quotas are tradeable, so companies that pollute less than they are permitted can sell their excess quotas to those who need them. Emissions trading is theoretically a transfer of wealth from polluters to nonpolluters.

However, the first phase of the ETS was a failure, principally because the national allocations were set far too high and therefore there was no pressure to cut emissions. The next phase will be crucial. The allocations need to be realistic, and the permits need to be auctioned, not merely handed out to companies. If industries have to pay for their quotas, they will be far more likely to value and act on them. It is also crucial that more sectors are included in the ETS. The scheme currently covers only 45% of all emissions including power plants, steel, cement and paper manufacturing. Aviation is excluded, along with manufacturers of aluminium and chemicals, and that clearly has to change.

Finally, we need also a fresh approach to regulation. Direct controls force polluting industries to improve their performance, and can eliminate products or practices deemed particularly hazardous from the market altogether. Such legislation delivers a known environmental outcome, and constitutes a powerful way of making companies mitigate their environmental impacts through the threat of fines or other repercussions. Markets without regulation would not have delivered unleaded petrol, for instance, or catalytic converters. Without regulations requiring smokeless fuel, London's smogs would still be with us.

Similarly, without new regulations, there can be no doubt that we will exhaust the world's fish stocks. It is hard to imagine sustainable fishing, for instance, while 60-mile-long lines are permitted, or purse seine nets, some of which are 1 km long, 200 m deep and big enough to engulf two Millennium Domes if placed one on top of the other. These tools of destruction are fundamentally incompatible with a sustainable future, and should simply be banned.

The reason that hasn't happened is that politicians fear taking on powerful vested interest. Consider the *Atlantic Dawn*, the world's biggest fishing vessel. It has purse seine nets with drawstring necks, 3,600 feet in circumference and 550 feet deep. Its trawl nets are 1,200 feet in breadth and 96 feet in height. It can process up to 400 tonnes of fish a day and can store up to 7,000 tonnes of frozen fish, grossing about $2m for each full fishing trip. So huge is the vessel that the Irish government had to encourage the EU to change its fishing rules to allow the *Atlantic Dawn* in European waters.

Regulations are key. But the regulatory approach needs to be strategic. With some products and processes, the regulatory bar needs to be raised internationally to avoid companies chasing the lowest standards globally. We also need a change in the regulatory approach, away from an obsessive policing of processes towards a focus on outcomes. If the regulatory system is too prescriptive, there is no room for innovation, and no real prospect of higher environmental standards.

The alternative is an approach based on trust. The government should set high standards but not dictate how they should be met. By pulling back, assuming the best instead of expecting the worst, the government would be freeing farmers, traders, providers and businesses to innovate. This approach works, but only if the government has the strength to step in heavily where trust is abused. The effect would be fewer, but more strategic and workable regulations and a corresponding increase in innovation and standards.

Two hundred years ago, Edmund Burke said:[4]

Society is a partnership not only between those who are living, but between those who are living, those who are dead, and those who are to be born. Each contract of each particular state is but a clause in the great primeval contract of eternal society.

It is difficult to imagine a more sensible approach, nor one further removed from that of our current political leaders.

British politicians, and the British people, have it within them to rise to this challenge. They have done it before. In 1939, a whole generation fought what seemed like an impossible battle – and won. After victory, in 1945, that generation joined with an unprecedented, government-led mission to build a pioneering welfare state, which lifted millions out of poverty and revolutionized the lives of ordinary people. The disaster of war spurred us on to create new priorities, and build a better country. Today, the impending ecological disaster gives us the chance to rise once again to the challenge.

The country needs leadership from its politicians, but they will not provide it unless we – the electorate – send them a clear message. For doing the right thing, they will be rewarded, and for doing the wrong thing, they will be sacked. In a democracy, it is for us to make that happen.

Now is the time to decide what sort of economy we want to develop from the ashes of this recession. Instead of struggling to recreate the conditions that delivered it, we can choose to stimulate the development of a cleaner, greener and much less wasteful economy. We can build something new, something that will regenerate our stagnant economy, and which, unlike the growth model that has dominated for decades, can actually last.

We ignored economists' warnings that we were living beyond our financial means. We cannot continue to ignore scientific warnings that we are exhausting nature's capital. As one US conservationist has cautioned: "Mother Nature doesn't do bailouts."

NOTES

1. *Ecosystems and Human Well-Being: Synthesis* (Millennium Ecosystem Assessment Series), Island Press, 2005, p. 1.

2. *TOPICS geo: Annual Review: Natural Catastrophes 2003*, Munich Reinsurance Group, Geoscience Research, Munich, p. 15, http://www.unisdr.org/eng/library/Literature/7638.pdf.

3. N. Stern, *The Economics of Climate Change: The Stern Review*, Cambridge, 2007.

4. E. Burke, *Reflections on the Revolution in France*, Oxford University Press, 1999, pp. 96–7.

9

THE FINANCIAL CRISIS AND THE END OF THE HUNTER-GATHERER*

Will Hutton

Plato first argued the case for proportionality – and it is telling that justice in so many cultures is signified by a pair of scales. Retribution should be proportional to the crime. But so should reward be proportional to our extra effort. It is a fundamental part of human beings' hard-wiring. The scales symbolically declare that justice is getting our due and proportional deserts.

The irony is that capitalism, if it is run properly, is a means for people to get just that. If they are a brilliant entrepreneur or innovator, then it is fair that they should get their proper due desert and make considerable, if proportional, profits. In fact, inventions are never the result of one individual light bulb moment, but the consequence of a lot of social and public investment. Thus, a proportion of the profit should go to the state as taxation, as its due desert for having collectively invested in the infrastructure and cumulative stock of knowledge from which invention draws – not least so that it can repeat the exercise for the next generation. But the big point is that big rewards are justifiable if they are in proportion to big efforts – because big effort grows the economic pie for everyone. Profit is ethical to the extent it is proportionate to effort and not due to good luck or use of brute power.

Taxation is ethical to the extent it is proportional to what the state has collectively provided.

There has been a financial crisis so severe it very nearly brought the Anglo-American financial system to its knees – but it has left little mark at all on how capitalism is understood by those at the top. For them, the paragraph above remains double Dutch. Instead, they like to characterize themselves as individualistic hunter-gatherers, being able to eat what they kill – and if they kill more than the next man or woman, they get to eat more. My property is my own because I and I alone have sweated my brow to get it; I have autonomy over it and no claim to share it, especially by the state, is legitimate. This is the cult of the investment banker or financial trader out to cut the next big deal or be a nanosecond faster than their competitor to buy or sell some financial instrument. It is only fair, they argue, that half a bank's revenues should be paid out in bonuses after each year's trading. The hunter-gatherers have to divide the kill once a year – and the annual bonus fest is a kind of primitive celebration of their prowess.

Yet, at the same time, they can rouse themselves into a state of fury about public debt – using the same visceral arguments about others that they would never apply to themselves. Debt is mortgaging the future. Debt is a means of unfairly living high on the hog today only to pay a bigger bill tomorrow. Of course, some borrowing is more morally justifiable than others. Borrowing to buy an asset like a home or to fix an unanticipated piece of bad luck like dry rot in the basement is more than justifiable. What is amoral is to try to escape the limits of what one fairly earns, worse still to pass the bill onto your children. It is to find a way of getting more than your due desert – the state behaving, well, as a banker might. Except at least it is borrowing for the public good.

But in the banker world, public debt is having our future mortgaged for us. It is public imprudence and public living beyond one's means. If, on top, the annual public deficit is the largest in Britain's peacetime history – as it was in 2009–10 – and it has been delivered by a discredited Labour government under a prime minister widely held to dissimulate to the point of outright dishonesty, then moral concern swells to outrage. A stage army of extraordinarily highly paid City executives insists that Britain cannot go on like this. The public deficit must be cut as a matter of moral urgency, more deeply and faster than the government plans.

They apply a morality to public debt they would never apply to themselves. But good economics attempts to deliver a functioning economic system that works for all its members. Necessarily, credit and debt play crucial economic functions, allowing the system to manage the inevitable mismatches between flows of revenue and costs over time. Changes in public debt are a vital instrument to manage the economy efficiently and, crucially, morally and fairly. Bystanders may think that the battle between 60 economists who signed letters to the *Financial Times* repudiating the 20 who earlier signed a letter to the *Sunday Times* urging that Britain's public deficit be eliminated over the course of a Parliament is a battle over economics. It is not. Economics is on the side of the 60. The gulf is about the morality of debt.

The *Sunday Times* 20 are less economists, and more, like the Tories, debt moralists. Underneath their unsubstantiated claim that currency and interest rate crises are inevitably associated with high public debt, so that recovery will be menaced, lay the scarcely concealed language of morality. By declaiming that the deficit was the largest in peacetime history, without placing it in the context of the biggest-ever recession, the inference was clear. A government that needed to regain trust was immorally taking debt to exceptional levels without good reason. Budgetary propriety had to be restored fast.

The hunter-gatherers are insisting on their pound of flesh, and of the inadmissibility of public endeavor, the common interest and shared risk. But even hunter-gatherers worked in packs and teams. And we also know that they quickly worked out the role of luck in being successful. They might not find animals to kill, not because they were not good hunters but because, unaccountably, there were no animals to kill. But if they returned to the cave empty-handed, they would expect to share in some other hunters' kill. Cooperation and a fair hand out of the spoils was an essential part of the hunter-gatherers' existence – if only for survival's sake.

The primitives knew that if you don't run an economy and society fairly, it quickly becomes dysfunctional, but this is not part of the world-view or culture of today's bankers. Lloyd Blankfein, CEO of Goldman Sachs, defends the astonishing earnings he and his colleagues, along with other investment bankers, make as "God's work". The logic is that society needs risk-taking bankers to generate credit flows, finance entrepreneurial enterprise and generally grow the economic pie for all. We should be grateful that they have got back on their feet so quickly; and grateful that they are prospering. So, in time, will all of us. If they make fabulous returns, this is proportional to their effort and contribution – just as football stars make fabulous returns.

This set of propositions, for so long uncontested, is a series of self-serving half-truths. Why are bankers able to get so much more reward for their proportional and extra effort than any other profession or occupation? Is the economic value added in making a loan, buying a share or securitizing an income stream so much greater than building a jet engine, creating a life-saving drug or writing a transformatory piece of new software? People work hard in many walks of life and cannot dream of earning what a banker earns. Moreover, the trading in money is not so much more valuable than any other form of economic activity that it deserves such privileges. This is not God's work. It is an old-fashioned market rigged by a bunch of smart insiders who have managed to get away with it for decades because hard questions were never asked about fairness or proportionality. And to add insult to injury, when the sky fell in on what was a gigantic Ponzi scheme, it was governments, backed by ordinary taxpayers, that launched a bailout to save the economy – but in the process also saved the bankers.

Of course intellectual mistakes were made about risk management techniques. Assumptions were made about economic behavior that proved wholly wrong. But at the heart of the financial crisis – and the criticism of the recovery – lay disregard for fairness. The bankers cast themselves as hunter-gatherers who owed nothing to anybody and could eat what they killed, careless of tomorrow. Banks carelessly ran down the capital at the core of their balance sheets, not replenishing and adding to it – but paying it out in dividends and bonuses. The Bank of England calculates that if, between 2000 and 2007, they had paid out just 20% less, they would have reserved more than the state paid out in bailout capital.

A credit default swap, allegedly insuring a security from the risk of default, is not a fair transaction if the insurer has no idea about the security's creditworthiness and is doing no more than issuing odds on a bet. A bank is not fair if it sells a buyer an asset whose promise to pay interest cannot be met because it depends upon subprime mortgages. It is not fair to bet ordinary depositors' savings on gambling in the derivative markets. It is not fair to press for rules to be changed to allow all this knowing that the state will pick up the tab when and if things go wrong. It is not fair to pay such high bonuses knowing that the bank is becoming riskier and riskier. And it is not fair to pay such high bonuses in recovery when the whole system has only survived courtesy of the taxpayer – hardly due desert for discretionary effort.

Now, to add insult to injury, the same folk apply a crooked morality to attack the growth of public debt that is the consequence of the recession they created. Three key linked economic arguments offer a different context to view the necessary growth of public debt, and thus morality. The first is best set out in a January 2010 paper from McKinsey Global Institute, "Debt and deleveraging: the global credit bubble and its economic consequences".[1] The authors have analysed 45 countries since 1930 after credit crises. Every one has been followed by a period of six to seven years in which consumers and companies reduce their debt on average by a quarter. Five countries – the US, the UK, Spain, South Korea and Canada – are now certain to go through the same painful process, if history is any guide. Because Britain has the most proportional private debt, it is the most acutely at risk. The process has hardly begun, but it will mean a prolonged period of very low growth in private demand – economically devastating.

How best to respond? The high priests of fiscal conservatism in recent decades have been the officials at the International Monetary Fund in Washington, but a paper whose authors included Emanuele Baldacci and Sanjeev Gupta, deputy division chief and deputy director of the Fiscal Affairs Division of the IMF, had a striking conclusion.[2] They examined 118 episodes of financial crises in 99 countries between 1980 and 2008, when, on average, national output fell by 5%, and found that while loosening monetary policy was vital to limiting the impact of recession, so was fiscal policy, the economists' term for spending, borrowing and taxing. Increasing borrowing by 1% of national output reliably reduces the length of recessions by two and a half months. The best response is increasing capital spending; lift that by 1% of national output and not only are recessions shorter, there is a permanent boost to economic growth of around a third of 1%.

The third argument to complete the chain is that, despite fears, Britain is financially capable of using fiscal policy as it has. Here is my last exhibit – the *IFS Green Budget* by the Institute for Fiscal Studies.[3] In partnership with economists from Barclays Bank led by Simon Hayes, the IFS paints a bleak picture of miserable 2% growth over the next decade. It observes that consumers are already doing what the McKinsey Global Institute predicts – saving and paying off debts. It is plain that if public demand fell any faster than the government plans for halving the deficit over four years outlined by Alistair Darling in 2009, then growth would be even lower. But, as the forecasters say, fortunately debt service is within the margins of safety, never rising above 10% of tax revenues even at the peak moment for public debt in 2014–15. It started from a low base and interest rates are very low. The IFS also remarks that whatever the credit rating agencies may say, Britain has not defaulted on its debt since the fourteenth century. There is zero risk today.

The next decade is going to be very tough, with huge economic risks. Debt moralists dominating the national debate do not help. It is difficult enough delivering good economic policy. Let's not make it even more difficult by making a blinkered morality rather than economics the compass for what the next government does. That way lies perdition.

Bankers and their apologists understood none of this then, and little of it now. They have a tin ear to fairness. But that was the consequence of allowing markets to be as rigged and gerrymandered as the financial markets have been – with no leverage caps, no rules on derivatives trading, easily circumvented rules on capital and an anything goes attitude to financial trading. Capitalism was run abusing all the principles of fairness. When cave dwellers were unfair, they died. When capitalism is unfair, we have financial crashes. Ethics and justice, it turns out, are the indispensable values to underpin successful capitalism. They were neglected and the crisis broke over our heads. Managing our way out will require that they are once again respected.

NOTES

*   This chapter has been adapted by Will Hutton from articles that he wrote for the *Observer* and the *Guardian* in February 2010.

1.   McKinsey Global Institute, "Debt and deleveraging: the global credit bubble and its economic consequences", January 2010, http://www. mckinsey.com/mgi/publications/debt_and_deleveraging/index.asp.

2.   C. Mulas-Granados, E. Baldacci and S. Gupta, *How Effective is Fiscal Policy Response in Systemic Banking Crises?*, IMF Working Papers, 09/160, 2009.

3.   R. Chote, C. Emmerson and J. Shaw (eds) *The IFS Green Budget*, doi: 10.1920/co.ifs.2010.0112, February 2010.

INDEX